Revise for GCSE Geography NEAB A

John Smith

Heinemann Educational Publishers
Halley Court, Jordan Hill, Oxford OX2 8EJ
A division of Reed Educational and Professional Publishing Ltd

Heinemann is a registered trade mark of
Reed Educational & Professional Publishing Ltd

OXFORD   MELBOURNE   AUCKLAND
JOHANNESBURG   BLANTYRE   GABORONE
IBADAN   PORTSMOUTH NH (USA)   CHICAGO

First published 1998

01 00
10 9 8 7 6 5 4

British Library Cataloguing in Publication Data
A catalogue record for this book is available from the British Library

ISBN 0 435 10138 2

Typeset and designed by Magnet Harlequin, Oxford
Printed and bound in Great Britain by the Bath Press, Bath

Acknowledgements
The publishers would like to thank the following for permission to
reproduce copyright material.

Science Photo Library/NOAA (p. 71 photo)

The publishers have made every effort to trace the copyright holders, but if
they have inadvertently overlooked any, they will be pleased to make the
necessary arrangements at the first opportunity

Contents

How to use this book

One of the great advantages of studying Geography is that it is all about real places and real processes. We can see geography going on in the world around us all the time. When we study geography we can go out into the field, or we can look at photographs, videos, satellite images, etc. and actually see what we are studying. We can marvel at wonderful and strange places – but we can also find much that is interesting about more familiar, local, everyday places. That does create some problems, though. The world is a very large place. No one can travel to see it all, and no one can study it all.

Geographers therefore try to see **patterns** in what they observe. All cities have certain things in common; all climates are linked together by the circulation of the winds; all rivers erode, transport and deposit material; and so on. Geographers have developed a series of key concepts or **key ideas** or theories to describe these patterns. When they know the key ideas well they can predict many things about new places, because they fit patterns that have already been studied. There are also special features about places, which make each one different from all other places. We have to study the patterns, but also the special features that make places unique and give them their 'sense of place'.

NEAB Syllabus A

This syllabus is divided into three **themes**:

- The challenge of urban environments
- Managing natural environments
- The impact of economic change.

Under each theme heading there are a series of **key ideas** (32 altogether). Each key idea must be studied at one or more of the following scales:

- local and small areas
- regional and national scale
- international scale
- global scale.

You must understand the key ideas, and then see how they apply to case studies of real places that you have studied. For most key ideas the syllabus does not tell you, or your teacher, which place should be studied. It leaves the choice of case studies open. Usually the teacher chooses a good example which (s)he knows well, or for which (s)he has good resources in a textbook or on a video. When the exam comes along you will be asked to explain the key idea, *with reference to a chosen example.*

Sense of place

In your answer it is essential to give detailed knowledge of a place that you have studied. You must show that you know about particular places – that is, that you have a 'sense of place'. For instance, you could be asked about cities in LEDCs, with reference to a named example. As well as answering the actual question, you must give details about São Paulo, or Bombay, or Nairobi, or whatever case study you have used. You must show that you know precise details about that particular place. What does it have in common with other cities in LEDCs, for example, and what makes it special?

Hints and Tips!

Note that throughout this book the abbreviations LEDC and MEDC are used. These stand for 'less economically developed country' (LEDC) and 'more economically developed country' (MEDC). These abbreviations are used in all the NEAB syllabuses.

The structure of the assessment

There are three parts to the assessment for NEAB Syllabus A. **Paper 1** consists of objective text questions, often known as 'multiple choice questions'. These can be set on any part of the syllabus. This paper is worth 25 per cent of the final mark.

- The **Foundation** paper lasts for 1 hour and consists of 50 questions, each worth one mark. They should all be answered.

- The **Higher** paper also lasts for 1 hour but consists of 60 questions, also worth one mark each. They should all be answered.

- Some questions will be on both the Foundation paper and the Higher paper.

- Note that questions which have been on a paper set by NEAB can be set on another paper at least three years later. This helps to check how standards in the exam compare between different year-groups. It also means that careful revision of past papers is very useful.

Paper 2 consists of structured questions which can be set on any part of the syllabus. Some sections need short answers, or ticking of boxes or underlining words. Other questions have to be answered by extended writing. One question will be based on an Ordnance Survey map. Detailed knowledge of case studies will be required in this paper. The paper is worth 50 per cent of the final mark.

- The **Foundation** paper lasts for 2 hours. It contains more short-answer sections and fewer sections needing extended writing.

- The **Higher** paper also lasts for 2 hours. It asks for more extended writing and contains fewer short-answer questions.

- Some parts of questions may be on both the Foundation and the Higher papers.

Coursework consists of a single geographical enquiry. It is worth 25 per cent of the final mark. It is not tiered.

How does this book use case studies?

Case studies form a very important part of all geography courses. They are studies of real places. They illustrate the key ideas that also form part of the course. For example, when you are studying glaciated landscapes, you look at:

- general ideas about how ice erodes

- general ideas about the formation of features like corries, arêtes and U-shaped valleys

- examples of these features and the way they fit together to form a landscape – for example you could study the Helvellyn region of the Lake District as a case study to show how the processes have formed a real place.

Essential specific knowledge
Some revision books give detailed case studies for the whole Geography GCSE course. This book only gives a small number of detailed studies. These are for parts of the syllabus which state that specific knowledge is essential (for example oil in Alaska; limestone scenery in National Parks). Most parts of the syllabus, though, do not specify which places should be studied. Key ideas are given which can be illustrated by any case study, and any good example can be used.

You have spent two years studying a set of case studies. If this book gave you a completely new set you could waste a lot of time. You would have to decide whether to learn your teacher's carefully chosen and planned examples which you have already studied or to use the new ones from the book. Learning new case studies at this stage of the course could mean a lot of extra work, and maybe create a lot of confusion too. So this book tries to help you to *use the examples from your class work in the most efficient way possible.*

Your own case studies
When you have to refer to one of your own case studies there is a box in the text headed '**Questions**'. This suggests what it is essential to learn from any relevant place you have studied. At this point you could:

- write notes in your notebook (or in this book, if it is your own)

- write a summary of your case study in your notebook or clip it into this book

- write down page references in your notebook or in this book, to show which page of your exercise or textbook contains the information needed.

Marginal notes

Special notes are included on the right-hand side of most pages in this book.

Hints and Tips!

These give general advice and useful information about how to prepare for and then sit the examination. Following this advice could stop you wasting time and effort *and* improve your grade.

These are useful facts and ideas that could provide helpful points in some of your exam answers.

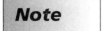 This is useful additional information about certain points in the text.

 One piece of advice for preparing for exams is: '**Active revision** (or doing things to help you remember) is usually better than **passive revision** (or just reading)'. The Focus Points give you little tasks to do to check that you are remembering what you have read.

Do the tasks set. They usually ask you what you can recall from the page or paragraph that you have just read. Jot down your answers in your notebook, or ask a friend or parent to test you. Be honest with yourself.

- If you do well you should be pleased.

- If you do badly, do not despair. Just re-read the section, but more carefully this time. Then test yourself again and hope to do better.

- You have tested your 'short-term memory'. How long will the information stick? Next time you come to do some revision you may well test yourself again. Renewing your revision like this often helps transfer the information into your medium or long-term memory, which is very important for the exam.

- Many of the Focus Points ask you for four or five facts. Often two or three will be enough in the exam. So why learn five?
  - It gives you something in reserve.
  - All the facts may not go into your long-term memory – but some will.
  - A full list of points helps you to *understand* as well as to learn.

Test questions

Some sections end with a test question, similar to the ones you may face in the exam. After each part of these questions there is a note like this:

(6 lines   3 marks)

This tells you how much space would be allowed to answer the question in the exam and the maximum marks you can hope to achieve. You may write extra, on the pages at the back of the exam booklet, but the space provides a rough guide to the amount of detail needed in your answer. If you write much more you may be wasting time. If you write much less your answer may lack detail.

Pages 125–127 give mark schemes, specimen answers and some advice on the best way to answer the questions – or sometimes on how not to answer them.

The multiple choice questions

Not every section has a test question at the end. When there is no test question, there are instead some multiple choice questions based on that topic, towards the end of the book (pages 121–123).

The multiple choice paper is an important feature of this syllabus. It worries some candidates, so there is a full section of advice on how to prepare for this paper, on pages 119–120. Note that it tests the same information and ideas as Paper 2, but in a different style. Some people are better at one style of question and some are better at the other. In the last few weeks before the exam, practise the paper that you are not so good at. Do not just concentrate on what you are comfortable with. Work hard on your areas of weakness.

Finally . . .

Good luck. Work hard, but . . .

- Try to enjoy your revision. It should be very satisfying to see the whole subject come together at the end of the course. You become a real geographer in this way, and real geographers impress examiners!

- Don't panic. Methodical, careful, steady work is far better than desperate over-cramming.

- Fit, relaxed, alert people do better in exams than burnt-out swotaholics.

- Pace yourself. Set yourself time for revision and time to have a break to go out or play sport or watch TV.

1 The challenge of urban environments

A Patterns and processes of urban growth

Key idea 1

An increasing percentage of the world's population lives in urban areas but the degree of urbanization varies.

Scale
Global

Expanded key idea

Urbanization means an increase in the proportion of the population living in cities and towns. It can also mean the movement of people from rural areas into cities and towns.

Where and why is urbanization taking place?

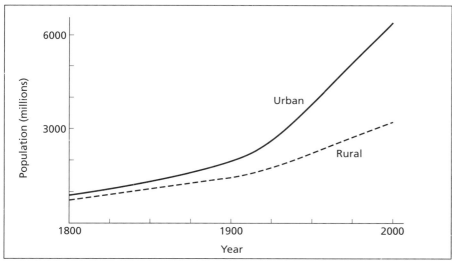

◀ *The growing proportion of the world's population living in urban areas*

Towns and cities have existed for about 10 000 years, but large-scale urbanization only really began around the start of the nineteenth century and the Industrial Revolution. The movement of people to cities followed the Industrial Revolution, with its demand for workers for the factories that developed. It took place throughout the nineteenth and early twentieth centuries in Europe and North America. By 1950 most of the population of those continents lived in urban areas. Urbanization then slowed down in most MEDCs, and now some of the biggest cities (like London) are losing population. This is known as **counterurbanization**.

Many people in MEDCs choose to live in the countryside – but only if they can still get into a city easily and quickly.

Since 1950 urbanization has taken place mainly in LEDCs in Latin America, Asia and Africa. On a world-wide scale it is possible to see that there are several causes of this change:

- Total population has grown rapidly because death rates have fallen but birth rates have stayed high.

- People have been 'pushed' to leave the countryside by such things as droughts and famine, mechanization, lack of opportunity, etc.

- They are 'pulled' to the cities by the hope of well-paid jobs, the greater opportunities to find casual or 'informal' work, better education, health care and entertainment, etc.

- In LEDCs most new investment takes place in cities – usually capital cities. New factories, ports, airports, offices, universities and so on are found in cities, and these all need workers – from scientific researchers and managers to cleaners and security guards. Most opportunities are found in cities.

Growth of 'million cities'
In most LEDCs urbanization is concentrated in one or two major cities. This has led to the development of 'million cities' (those with over a million inhabitants) in many of these countries.

In 1950 most of the biggest cities were in Europe and North America. By 2010 most will be in South America and Asia.

Focus Point 1

Cover up the page. Give four common 'pushes' and four common 'pulls' that encourage rural-to-urban migration in LEDCs.

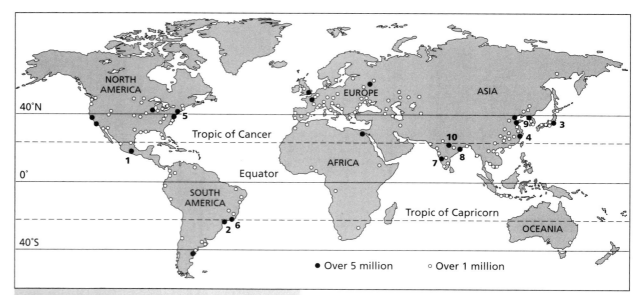

- Over 5 million   ○ Over 1 million

▲ *The world's ten biggest cities*

1	Mexico City	6	Rio de Janeiro
2	São Paulo	7	Bombay
3	Tokyo	8	Calcutta
4	Shanghai	9	Seoul
5	New York	10	Delhi

Focus Point 2

Learn the names of the world's five biggest cities. Then learn where to mark them on a world map.

The graph shows how rapidly the world distribution of 'million cities' has changed since 1940.

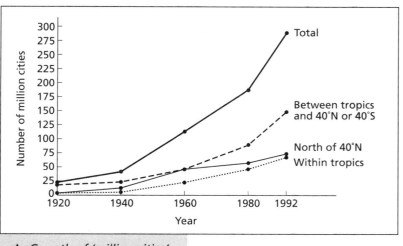

▲ *Growth of 'million cities'*

ocus
Point 3

Check Focus Point 1 again. Did you give 'opposites' like 'few jobs/lots of jobs'? That will not get top marks. 'Loss of jobs because of mechanization/ jobs in industry' is better.

Most of the world's fastest-growing cities are:

- in LEDCs
- between 40°N and 40°S of the equator
- in south and south-east Asia, Latin America or Africa
- near the coast.

Questions

1 For a case study of a named city in an LEDC, list three push factors and three pull factors that have helped to cause the growth of that city.

2 Make sure that your factors are specific. For example, if you were dealing with São Paulo's pull factors:
   - 'Jobs' may be true, but it is vague.
   - 'Jobs in industry' is a little better.
   - 'Jobs in the motor industry, with firms like VW and Fiat' is splendid.
   - 'Some formal sector jobs, with car makers like Fiat and VW' is magnificent.

Problems of urban life

Key idea 2   **Scale**

Urbanization is one cause of the problems of urban life. The nature of these   *Local*
problems and their solutions vary according to socio-economic, historical and   *Regional*
political factors.   *National*

Expanded key idea

Cities are places where many people find opportunities for work and a more fulfilling life.
Many problems are also found mainly in cities. However, these problems can be tackled by
the authorities, by individuals and by groups of people working together.

Housing in MEDCs

Nineteenth-century rapid urbanization

In nineteenth-century Europe and North America the rapid growth of
cities led to many problems. These included the following.

- Unemployment and low wages – at times urbanization was faster
  than industrialization. People moved but jobs were not available.

- Slum housing – factory owners built cheap houses as close to their
  works as possible. They were often poorly built and very crowded.

- Poor hygiene – water supply and sewerage systems could not be
  built fast enough to keep pace with urban growth.

- Lack of open space – houses were crowded together with no room
  for private gardens or public open space.

- Air pollution – coal-powered factories and houses heated with coal
  fires helped pollute the air, causing lung diseases.

Turn-of-the-century solutions

In the late nineteenth and the twentieth centuries, these problems were
tackled. In Britain, work by national and local government, trade
unions, enlightened factory owners and reforming individuals led to
improved conditions in the towns and cities. Changes were brought
about by:

- Public Health Acts, which compelled city authorities to build
  sewerage systems, etc.

- development of 'model' factories and well-designed workers'
  housing, by mill owners like Robert Owen and Titus Salt

- Factory Acts, passed by parliament, making working conditions
  much safer

- slum clearance and the building of council housing by local authorities

- planning of new housing areas to include both public and private
  open spaces.

New housing solutions in the 1960s and 1970s

Very widespread slum clearance and building of new houses took place in Britain in the 1960s and 1970s. Unfortunately, the demand for new houses was great but the resources available were limited. Ways had to be found to redevelop housing as cheaply as possible. Some of the solutions to the problem were:

- building high-rise flats, to fit as many people as possible into a small area

- building council estates on the edges of towns, where the land was cheaper

- 'systems building' – that is, using sections of buildings that are partly made up in factories, then bolted together on site

- building estates without private gardens but with communal open space, which could be used by everybody.

These schemes provided houses with better amenities than the slums. They had hot and cold running water, and proper kitchens and bathrooms. Many new developments were in attractive areas with pleasant views, close to open space and the countryside. They had good public transport connections into the city centres.

Problems of new housing

But many of the developments were built too cheaply and quickly. The design of the flats and houses, and the layout of estates, soon started to produce new problems such as:

- 'new town blues' – young mothers found themselves isolated in new communities, cut off from friends and relations

- damp – caused by poor ventilation in the new designs of housing

- vandalism – young people, bored by life on new estates with few facilities, looked for new ways of getting their excitement

Hints and Tips!

You can learn a lot about urban growth by looking out of the bus, car or train window as you travel into a town centre.

 **ocus Point 1**

Cover up the page. Give two reasons why the new estates were better than the old slums. Give two reasons why they were worse.

Questions

Housing in MEDCs

This section has dealt with:
- the development of towns in nineteenth-century Britain
- planning to deal with rapid urbanization
- new housing solutions in the 1960s and 1970s
- further problems caused by the 'solutions'.

1   Look back at your own case studies. Add references to any examples that illustrate some of these points.

2   You may add further points – again with references to your own case studies.

3   Finally, refer to recent developments in your case study areas where attempts are being made to deal with the new problems.

- insecurity – on estates that were designed with many dark corners and hiding places, but with no real privacy

- unsafe housing – caused by using new materials such as concrete which crumbled, and asbestos which caused lung damage.

Traffic in MEDCs

The growth of urban areas has always depended on transport systems to move people and goods into and out of the area, and to move them around within the area. Since the Industrial Revolution, changing technology has brought changes to the transport systems. These have had big effects on most towns in Britain.

Canals
- These developed after about 1780.

- They were used to carry coal and bulky raw materials.

- They were also used to carry fragile finished goods, like pottery, which needed a smooth journey.

- Industry was attracted to the canal banks, and to basins where barges moored.

Railways
- From 1840 onwards these replaced canals for most movements of freight.

- There was a better network serving more towns than canals did.

- Lines were built to mines, ports, etc.

- Industry, especially heavy industry, was attracted to locate near the railways. It became concentrated around stations, close to city centres.

- Passengers could be carried by train. Journeys were much quicker than by any other available transport.

- Many people travelled into town centres by rail, from suburbs and villages. These were the first 'commuters'. This allowed towns to start spreading outwards as people no longer had to live within walking distance of work.

- Railways also allowed seaside resorts to develop, as people could travel from industrial towns for days out, or even to stay on holiday.

- By 1965 car ownership had become widespread and many railway lines were closed, especially the smaller branch lines. Short journeys by rail were no longer economic. Travelling by train was not as convenient as travelling by car. Since 1965 a lot of old railway land has become available for redevelopment close to city centres.

Roads
Most towns developed around meeting places of roads, where markets were held. Many town centres still show the effects of the old road pattern, with narrow, winding streets, not designed for cars. Some streets widen out to provide space for the old market.

Hints and Tips!

Learn to draw a map of your case study town or city, with CBD, station, railway, about four main roads and about five features illustrating different stages of its growth.

- Car ownership started to become common in the 1930s, causing 'ribbon development' – the spread of middle-class housing along roads leading out of town.

- Car ownership boomed from the 1960s onwards, and had a massive influence on the layout of towns. Roads converged in town centres causing much congestion.

- Many old buildings were demolished to allow for road widening. Car parks were built, but they are expensive.

- Inner ring roads were built to keep traffic out of town centres.

- Outer ring roads and by-passes were built to keep through traffic out of towns.

- One-way schemes, underpasses, peak flow lanes and other local schemes were designed to cope with city centre traffic.

- Large numbers of cars, and the stop-start travel in towns, causes air pollution.

- Congestion in town centres caused factories to be moved to the outskirts, especially to ring roads, where lorry access is easier.

- New shopping centres have been built on the edges of towns. Car parking is easier here than in the centre, and free.

Public transport changes

- One bus can carry as many people as several cars, so the use of buses cuts down congestion and pollution. Many councils try to encourage the use of buses, by park-and-ride schemes, bus priority lanes, increasing the price of car parking, etc.

- Commuter railway systems and tramways have been re-introduced in some cities, although they are very expensive to build, e.g. Tyneside Metro, Sheffield Supertrams.

Focus Point 2

Cover up the page. List four ways in which town centres have had to change to cope with cars. Try to think of specific examples of changes from your case studies.

Focus Point 3

Which groups in society rely more on public transport than on cars (young/middle-aged/old/male/female/rich/poor/able-bodied/infirm/middle-class/working-class)? Should this affect transport policy?

Hints and Tips!

Some people worry about using their own local area as a case study in an exam. They fear the examiner will not know the area, so will not them give good marks. Don't worry! Examiners have clear instructions to award marks if candidates show local knowledge.

Questions

Changes in transport

Refer to your case study of a town or city in an MEDC.

1 Name places that fit ideas in the lists above.

2 How have changes in the types of transport led to changes in the layout of the town?

Housing in cities in LEDCs

The population of cities in many LEDCs has grown very fast, and is still growing. It is well known that there are not enough properly built houses for all the new migrants. Many people have to live in 'spontaneous settlements' which they build for themselves. To people like us, who live in 'proper houses' in MEDCs, the condition of these settlements looks appalling – but it is vital that geography students understand why and how these settlements were built, and what goes on there.

Most people are attracted to the cities because they are places of opportunity. Many newcomers cannot get formal jobs, but they can make a living in the informal sector. (This does not just mean shoe-shining. It includes a great variety of work: buying and selling, making and mending, servicing and recycling.) The chance of an education for the children of such people offers a further opportunity for the family to get on. People in this situation have to be very flexible and adapt to change, if they are to survive and prosper. They need a home, but they do not need luxury.

Many GCSE students write about spontaneous settlements with a very stereotyped view of the squalor and poverty. They often miss out the **reasons** for the conditions that they describe.

Hints and Tips!

Case studies seen on video are easy to remember – but not every boy in São Paulo works as a shoe-shiner!

ocus Point 4

Cover up the page. Give five negative stereotypes of spontaneous settlements. Give the reasons why settlements develop like this.

Negative stereotypes	Reasons
• Houses are poorly built, often using scrap material.	Money is in short supply. It has to be spent on food, or invested in tools or materials for work.
• Houses seem to be poorly planned, with bits tacked on.	Homes have to provide a place for the family to sleep and eat – and the family may change size as children are born but others go off to work elsewhere; relatives from the home village may need support when they first arrive in the city.
• There are no proper windows, and walls are very flimsy.	Many LEDCs are in the tropics. Ventilation may be more important than insulation.
• They do not have proper toilets and sewers.	These services are expensive and complicated. They may be provided in the future, but people often make latrines by digging pits, which are emptied by tanker lorries every few months.
• They do not have electricity.	Once settlements have become established the authorities often link them up to the supply – but it is difficult to keep pace with the rapid growth.
• There are no roads, only dirt tracks.	Not many people own cars. It is more important to have access to a bus route to the city centre.
• The area looks a mess.	Many people are carrying on their jobs in and around their homes. Builders have to store materials, some keep animals for food, others make things from recycled scrap to sell on the streets, and so on. Opportunity is more important than tidiness.

All the people who live in spontaneous settlements do not stay in them for ever. Some make enough money to buy properly built houses, some move back to the countryside, some marry and move away, and so on. In addition, all cities have some schemes for rehousing people in properly built homes. For instance:

- Site and service schemes – the authorities provide water and sewerage systems, and people build their own homes, e.g. as in São Paulo.

- Upgrading – the authorities gradually provide running water, main drains, electricity and street lighting for settlements, e.g. as in Malawi and some other African countries.

- Intermediate technology – simple technology is used to improve people's homes. For instance, small moulds for making breeze-blocks were provided in Santa Marta, Colombia; and people in southern India were shown how to improve thatched roofs using a waterproof compound made from cashew nut resin.

- Relocation (in wealthier countries, such as Hong Kong) – involves moving people to new, cheap housing. This is often in tower blocks, either close to the CBD or on the edges of the built-up areas.

Exam practice

Name a city in a less economically developed country that has attracted many new migrants.

(a) Explain why migrants have come to the city. (Refer to push and pull factors.) (6 lines 4 marks)

(b) Describe how the new migrants find housing, even though there may be a shortage of housing in the city. (10 lines 6 marks)

(c) Many people in cities in LEDCs work in the 'informal sector'. What does this mean? (6 lines 4 marks)

Hints and Tips!

It is difficult to avoid the stereotypes. Many textbooks describe cities in LEDCs in very general terms. However, you should try to:

- know specific facts about named cities and

- find detailed examples of case studies that describe individual settlements, rather than just making big general statements.

B Patterns of land use

Key idea 1

Scale

There is a tendency for similar land users, both residential and non-residential, to concentrate in distinct areas of cities.

Local
Regional
International

Expanded key idea

The land in cities is used for many different purposes: housing, industry, shopping, transport, leisure, other services, etc. Some of these different types of **land use** become concentrated in certain areas of cities. For example, some areas consist mainly of shops, other areas are mostly industrial, and large parts are used mainly for housing.

The central business district (CBD)

CBDs in most cities developed around the most accessible area. This was usually where several roads met, and near to railway and bus stations. When cities first started to grow there was usually a market-place near the centre. The market-place may still be there, but now most CBDs are dominated by offices and large shops.

- CBDs are very busy areas.

- People can get to them easily from all directions.

- Because CBDs are accessible there are lots of customers for businesses located there.

- This makes businesses in this area very profitable, so many firms want to locate in the CBD.

- Rents in CBDs are usually higher than in other parts of cities.

- Buildings are built high so that as many firms as possible can locate in the CBD.

- Businesses attract more and more customers until the CBD becomes so congested that business starts to decline (see page 13).

Hints and Tips!

In examinations you should usually avoid abbreviations, but 'CBD' is so common that it is safe to use it in geography.

**ocus Point 1**

Cover up the page. Explain why rents of shops in CBDs are usually high.

Questions

The central business district

For a case study city, draw a sketch map which shows:
- some routes into the CBD including some of the following: roads, railway lines, underground or metro lines, train and bus stations, major car parks, etc.
- the main shopping street(s), possibly including major department stores, pedestrian streets, or undercover shopping centres
- some of the main office areas
- other major features, such as a cathedral, football ground, town hall, etc.

Industrial areas in cities

After the Industrial Revolution, factories developed in most towns and cities. During the nineteenth and early twentieth centuries they were concentrated in industrial areas close to the city centres. This was because they needed to be:

- close to sources of raw materials and fuel, especially coal, which were very bulky and difficult to transport

- close to canals, railways or ports, because the bulky raw materials arrived here

- close to the crowded areas of workers' houses, which were built as close as possible to most town and city centres.

Industries move out to the suburbs

After about 1930, transport by lorry started to become very important for some industries, especially new, light industry. The owners of the new factories wanted to avoid the crowded, old industrial areas. Many new factories were built along main roads leading out of the town centres. The new buildings were usually lighter and more spacious than the old factories. They were built fairly close to the new suburban housing that was spreading outwards from the city centres at this time.

The Hoover factory in the western suburbs of London was a very good example of this type of development. It was built by a modern American company, when vacuum cleaners were still a very new idea. It was designed to look very modern, to fit in with the image that Hoover was trying to project – clean, technical, efficient, and freeing people from drudgery.

As road transport became more and more important, new factories were built further and further away from the centres. Many new factories were built on industrial estates on the edges of towns and cities.

New industry that is not 'tied' to locations near to bulky raw materials is often described as 'footloose'.

Advantages of industrial estates	Disadvantages of inner city industrial sites
• Easy access to motorways, ring roads and by-passes	• Congested, with narrow roads built for smaller lorries and less road traffic
• A clean, attractive environment, close to open countryside and fresh air	• Old buildings in a noisy and often polluted environment
• Land is usually cheap	• Land is more expensive because of restricted area
• It is not expensive to make 'greenfield sites' fit for new building	• Expensive demolition and reclamation work is often needed on old 'brownfield' sites before new building can take place
• Many workers now live in estates on the urban fringe, or in commuter settlements outside the urban area	• The workers who lived in inner city areas have moved out, because of clearance and redevelopment, or because they can now afford houses in a pleasanter environment

Questions

Industrial areas in cities

For your case study town or city, name and describe:
- a nineteenth-century industrial area
- a mid-twentieth century, main road industrial area
- a late-twentieth century industrial estate.

For each example that you have named, give three reasons why it developed in that particular place.

Focus Point 2

Cover up the previous page. List four advantages of out-of-town sites for industry, and four disadvantages of inner city sites.

Housing areas in cities

In many cities, housing covers more land than all the other land uses. Many different types of housing can be recognized. Similar types of house are often found grouped together. Types of housing area can be classified according to:

- **age** – e.g. Victorian or nineteenth century, inter-war, 1945 to 1960, recent

- **cost** – this influences who can afford to live in the area

- **style** – includes such aspects as terraced/semi-detached/detached, etc.

- **building height** – low-rise (bungalows or two storeys) to high-rise blocks

- **density of population** – wealthier areas are usually low-density with lots of open space; poorer areas are often more crowded with less open space

- **ownership** or **type of tenancy** – including owner-occupied, private rented, rented from the council, or housing association

- **environmental quality** – includes the amount of open space, but also freedom from traffic, noise, air and water pollution; safety; state of repair of buildings and roads, etc.

Focus Point 3

Choose two or three housing areas that you are familiar with. Try to use at least four of the headings listed here, to describe the type of housing in each area.

As geography students you are mainly interested in where the different types of housing are found. Housing often changes as one moves away from the city centre towards the edge. The diagram below shows the pattern in general.

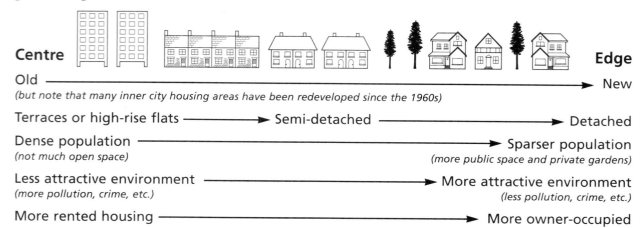

Centre .... **Edge**

Old ⟶ New
(but note that many inner city housing areas have been redeveloped since the 1960s)

Terraces or high-rise flats ⟶ Semi-detached ⟶ Detached

Dense population ⟶ Sparser population
(not much open space) *(more public space and private gardens)*

Less attractive environment ⟶ More attractive environment
(more pollution, crime, etc.) *(less pollution, crime, etc.)*

More rented housing ⟶ More owner-occupied
(and also more council estates)

Questions

Housing areas in cities

1 For your case study town or city, describe the types of housing found in named examples of:
   - inner city areas
   - inner suburbs
   - outer suburbs
   - rural/urban fringe.

2 Some cities are described as having 'concentric rings' of housing types. Others have 'sectors'. Does your case study fit either of these models?

This key idea can be studied with reference to any town or city that you choose. Most people will have studied examples from the UK. You also need to compare your UK example with a city in at least one LEDC and at least one other country in the European Union.

3 Name the cities you have studied for comparison:
   - in an economically less developed country
   - in an EU country.

4 Describe the layout of each city.

In your exam you should only be asked for details about the structure of **one** EU city and **one** LEDC city. Make sure you know these two case studies well.

Hints and Tips!

When you revise this topic, make sure you know the names of real estates and parts of the city. If you give real names it gives your answer a good 'sense of place'.

Exam practice

From your experience of urban geography, is it true to say that 'housing quality improves as you get further away from the city centre'?   (10 lines 6 marks)

Changes in land use

Key idea 2

Patterns of land use change. This challenges people, especially planners, to either maintain or improve the environment.

Scale

Local

Regional

Expanded key idea

Land use in towns and cities changes. The changes are caused by economic, technological and social change. Sometimes these changes can damage people's environment. Planners have to try to make sure that changes take place in the best way possible so that the needs of all groups in society are met.

Changes in technology bring changes in land use

Changing technology can bring many benefits. It can also cause problems. For example:

- New technology has made the transport of goods by sea more efficient.

- Examples include bulk carriers, container ships and more efficient ways of lifting goods off the ships and transferring them to road or rail transport.

- This brought many advantages, such as:
  - Ships can be unloaded more quickly.
  - Goods can be delivered to their destination faster and more reliably.
  - Old docks have been replaced by new docks in better locations.
  - There are fewer breakages and less damage to goods.
  - Hard, dangerous work has been replaced by machinery.
  - Some low-paid workers can be trained for better, higher-paid work.
  - Firms that develop and use the new technology can make big profits.

- But when developments like this happened in the United Kingdom in the 1960s and 1970s they caused very serious problems in old dockland areas like London and Liverpool. Problems included:
  - Many dock workers lost their jobs, especially older, less skilled men.
  - Many old buildings and docks were abandoned. This left ugly and dangerous areas.
  - People with jobs in the new dock areas often moved out of the old dockland areas.
  - As people with good jobs moved out, the old areas were left with fewer people earning good wages.
  - Shops and other businesses in the area lost customers and often had to close.
  - The area went into a downward spiral. Jobs and services were lost, the environment got worse, crime increased, and people lost hope.

A place where freight is unloaded from one form of transport and loaded onto another is called a 'break of bulk' point. Industry often develops here, to save on transport costs.

 **ocus Point 1**

Cover the page. Describe at least four stages of the run-down of an old inner city dockland area.

Questions

Changes in land use

1 Make reference to an example of an urban area that you have studied which has gone through a period of major change.

2 Describe what caused the change.

3 List some of the benefits and problems brought by the change.

4 Suggest which groups benefited from the changes, and which lost out.

The regeneration of urban areas

Often, when areas of decline have become very run down, a decision is made to try to improve the area. This improvement is called **regeneration**. Various different groups can take on the responsibility for regeneration. These can include:

- groups of local residents
- local authorities (e.g. town or county councils)
- the national government, which usually sets up special groups, for example Urban Development Corporations (UDCs)
- the European Union regional development organizations
- big firms and corporations which either already have investments in the area or which are interested in moving into the area.

Regeneration of areas often involves a number of these groups. It usually works best when groups work closely together.

In many places the European Union has provided some of the money that is needed to pay for regeneration. However, it does not plan what needs doing. The local or national government draws up plans, and then asks the EU for support.

An example of regeneration

For example, in Middlesbrough the local council and the government wanted to develop an old industrial area alongside the River Tees. They planned to build a barrage across the river to stop polluted water from industrial areas near the river mouth being washed upstream by the tide. Then they wanted to landscape the area and build new, high-tech industrial units in the pleasant environment. A new university campus was also included in the plans, and a whitewater canoeing course to attract leisure users to the area.

Now the plan is being carried out, using funds provided by the local council, the UDC, and the EU's regional development fund.

Gentrification

Gentrification is a process of redevelopment which has happened in some inner city areas, such as Islington in London. These were originally areas of working-class housing, close to the city centres. In

The EU Regional Development Fund tries to bring jobs to areas that have lost employment because they are isolated and not well placed to attract industry.

Focus Point 2

Describe Middlesbrough's development plan. Mention:
- pollution control
- industry
- education
- environment
- leisure
- funding.

recent years they have become fashionable, as young people who work in well-paid jobs in the city have bought these small terraced houses and 'done them up' so that they can live near to their work and to their city night life. Property prices have shot up. The working-class people have moved out and have been replaced by a 'young upwardly mobile' ('yuppie') population. Gentrification is not planned, but happens spontaneously because of decisions made by individuals.

Regeneration versus conservation

When planners are deciding how to develop areas in cities, they often see that there is a conflict between development and conservation.

Focus Point 3

Cover up the page. Describe three ways in which conflict between developers and conservationists may be resolved.

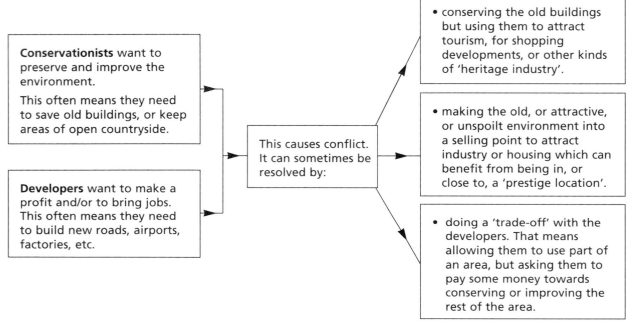

Conservationists want to preserve and improve the environment.
This often means they need to save old buildings, or keep areas of open countryside.

Developers want to make a profit and/or to bring jobs. This often means they need to build new roads, airports, factories, etc.

This causes conflict. It can sometimes be resolved by:

• conserving the old buildings but using them to attract tourism, for shopping developments, or other kinds of 'heritage industry'.

• making the old, or attractive, or unspoilt environment into a selling point to attract industry or housing which can benefit from being in, or close to, a 'prestige location'.

• doing a 'trade-off' with the developers. That means allowing them to use part of an area, but asking them to pay some money towards conserving or improving the rest of the area.

Of course things do not always work out nicely like this. Sometimes development, for profit and/or job creation, can cause great damage to the natural environment, to the previous built environment, or to local communities.

Questions

The regeneration of urban areas

1 Name a case study where planners have tried to improve the environment of part of a city.

2 Describe the changes that had caused the area to deteriorate, and the problems that arose because of these changes.

3 What was done, in this area, to try to improve conditions?

4 Were there any conflicts between different groups during the regeneration?

5 How successful do you think the regeneration has been?

In the 1960s, British cities were very badly damaged by planners and developers who destroyed many attractive old areas and built ugly new buildings. Some people said that the developers finished off the destruction of city centres that had begun during bombing raids in the Second World War.

C Dynamism in urban areas – migration

> **Key idea 1**
> Certain areas of cities are particularly attractive to newcomers. New migrants tend to concentrate in these areas.
>
> **Scale**
> *Local*
> *Regional*
> *International*
>
> **Expanded key idea**
> Many cities in the United Kingdom and other parts of the EU have attracted immigrants from LEDCs. When the first migrants arrived they had to find cheap housing, so they often settled in old inner city areas. As more people from the same places arrived they often moved into the same areas, because they could get help and support from their families and friends.

Urban structures

In most GCSE courses there is some reference to the Burgess model. He based it on a study of Chicago in the 1920s. He said cities develop in concentric rings.

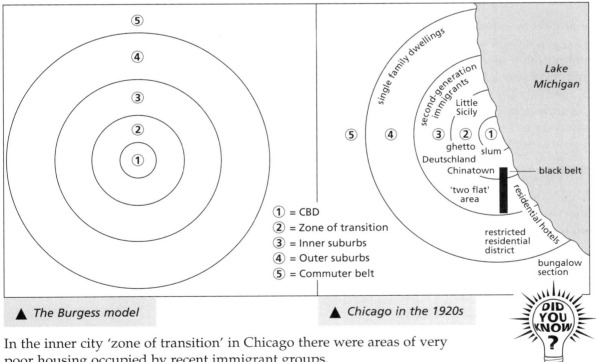

① = CBD
② = Zone of transition
③ = Inner suburbs
④ = Outer suburbs
⑤ = Commuter belt

▲ The Burgess model   ▲ Chicago in the 1920s

In the inner city 'zone of transition' in Chicago there were areas of very poor housing occupied by recent immigrant groups.

- 'Little Sicily' had many Italians, mainly from the poor south including Sicily.

- 'Chinatown' was home to Chinese migrants who had worked building the transcontinental railways.

- 'The ghetto' was largely inhabited by Jews from eastern Europe.

- 'The black belt' was only just starting to develop. Black Americans had started to move to the northern cities during the First World War.

DID YOU KNOW?

In the early part of this century, the USA was known as a 'melting pot' because it was thought that immigrants from all over the world could come and mix together to make 'America'.

Further out from the centre 'Deutschland' had many German families. Other areas had Scandinavians, Polish and Irish groups.

Case study

Why had these 'ethnic' areas developed?

Imagine a young Italian couple who had been forced to leave their village in Sicily because of desperate poverty. They had saved up enough money for a cheap voyage to America on an overcrowded boat. They had heard that the USA was 'the land of opportunity' but when they arrived in Chicago they had no money, no food and few clothes. They did not speak English. The only skills they had were those they had learned working on a farm in the Mediterranean climate region.

What could they do? They had to look for help and support from other Italian immigrants. Most newcomers to Chicago had the names of family or friends from their home village, who could help by:

- providing a room to stay in, at least while they 'found their feet'

- helping them to find a job

- showing them round and introducing them to other people

- helping them to understand the customs of the new country.

Most immigrants soon found jobs. The city's industry was growing fast, and there was a big demand for labour. Many employers encouraged immigration, because many newcomers were willing to do hard or dirty or poorly-paid jobs. Most people who had been born in Chicago were not willing to do these jobs, because they could get better-paid jobs elsewhere.

Reasons for staying
As the new immigrants started to get settled they often wanted to stay living in an area where there were other Italians (for example), because here there would be:

- cheap housing that could be rented by people on low wages

- people who could speak their language – people to talk and gossip to about 'home', restaurants serving Italian food, bars with Italian wine where Italian music was performed

- small businesses, run by Italians, who might offer jobs to other Italians

- Catholic churches, with priests who could take confession in Italian

- banks run by Italians, who would send money back home to help support the family in Italy

- organizations that protected Italian immigrants if they were threatened by other local groups – they might even protect them from what they saw as police harassment.

ocus Point 1

Name four groups who lived in inner city Chicago in the 1920s, and two groups who had moved out to the suburbs.

ocus Point 2

Name the main **push** factor and the main **pull** factor that made this couple move.

DID YOU KNOW?

'The Godfather' films may be fiction, but they give a good picture of what it must have been like for Italian immigrants in the USA at this time.

ocus Point 3

Give at least four reasons why new migrants into a city may wish to live near to people from their own ethnic group.

Ethnic areas therefore became very attractive places for new immigrants to live. This was why 'Little Sicily' developed in Chicago. Similar things happened in the Jewish and Chinese areas.

Reasons for leaving

After a few years many immigrants began to earn more money. They learned English, and began to fit in with the American way of life. Many decided they could afford to move out of the inner city areas and buy bigger, better houses in the suburbs. In the 1920s, when Burgess was writing, this had already happened with the Germans. Many of them had bought houses in the suburbs, but a lot of families still lived close to each other in the same suburb, known as 'Deutschland'.

By the 1940s and 1950s, Jewish and Italian families were moving out to the suburbs too. When they started to leave their inner city houses, other groups could move in – and just at this time there was large-scale migration of black Americans. The inner city was suitable for the black newcomers, just as it had been for the Italian immigrants. There was cheap housing, some jobs, and people with a similar background and culture. All this made the area safe and supportive to the new inhabitants.

Migration into cities in the UK

In the 1960s there was a shortage of workers in many industries in the UK. Workers were especially needed in the health service, transport, the textile industry and metalworking industry. Many companies advertised for workers in the West Indies and in the Indian sub-continent, which used to be British colonies. When the migrants arrived, many of them settled in groups in the old inner city areas where there was poor housing. These areas developed in a similar way and for similar reasons that the ethnic areas in cities in the USA had developed in the 1920s.

Focus Point 4

Name four industries that were short of labour in the UK in the 1960s and which were keen to employ immigrants from the Caribbean and south Asia.

Questions

Migration into cities in the UK

1 Name part of a town or city in the UK where immigrants have settled and say where the immigrants come from?

2 What are the main jobs that are available for people in that area?

3 What social, religious, educational and other services are there which can help new migrants settle in the area?

Now, about 30 years after the first large-scale migration of Asians and West Indians into the UK, some people have moved from their original homes in the inner cities. They are buying houses in the suburbs of many cities. This is similar to what Burgess observed in Chicago in the 1920s.

D The challenge of change in urban environments

Key idea 1

Scale
Local
Regional
International

Issues in the built environment result from the consequences of changes in transport and people's perception of environmental quality.

Expanded key idea

Since the end of the Second World War there have been many changes in the structure of cities. Many of these have resulted from changes in transport, particularly the decline of rail transport and the increase in road transport. At the same time people's ideas about what makes places attractive to live in have changed. The changes that have resulted include:

(a) the movement of people from inner cities out to the suburbs, and beyond
(b) changes to the areas where towns and cities meet the countryside
(c) changes to the rural environment
(d) redevelopment of old inner city areas
(e) changes in the location and character of shopping centres.

(a) The movement of people out from the city centres

Questions

Refer back to pages 12–13 and re-read the section on transport changes.

1 Pick out five points which show how changes in transport have allowed people to move and live away from the centres of towns and cities. Choose:
   • one point to do with railways
   • three points to do with roads
   • one point to do with public transport changes.

2 Now name a case study of an old, inner city area that you have studied.

3 Give four **push factors** that made people move away from that area.

4 Give four **pull factors** that attracted them to live nearer to the edge of the city.

The figures in the next table show how Manchester's population has changed. They are typical of what has happened in many other towns and cities in the UK.

Manchester's population

Year	Total population
1931	766 311
1951	703 082
1961	662 021
1971	543 859
1981	462 500
1991	438 500
1996	430 818

There were two main reasons for the changes.

1 There was a fall in the average size of households, partly due to falling birth rates. It was also partly due to young people leaving home earlier to start their own families and set up their own homes, often away from the city centres.

2 There was a decline in the number of houses in the city centre, due to slum clearance. Between 1951 and 1980, 83 255 houses were demolished in Manchester, and only 59 468 new ones were built in the city (23 344 houses were built by the council on overspill estates outside the city boundaries).

Between 1961 and 1980 the rates of decline in other English cities were:

Birmingham	−14.9%	Leeds	−1.1%
Liverpool	−31.6%	Manchester	−32.2%
Newcastle	−17.4%	Sheffield	−8.1%

(b) Changes to the areas where towns and cities meet the countryside

Middlesbrough is a town that has been losing population too, but these figures show how the number of households has risen, and is predicted to go on rising.

Middlesbrough's population

Year	1981	1991	2001 (est.)	2006 (est.)
Population	150 000	144 000	143 000	140 000
Households	54 000	55 600	57 800	58 300

People want more houses. They do not want to live in inner city areas. Therefore a lot of new houses have had to be built on **greenfield sites** on the edges of urban areas. The two maps on page 28 show how the built-up area of Middlesbrough has expanded southwards, into countryside. This has formed the new suburb of Coulby Newham. Most of the land here used to be farmland, although it was not very high quality.

◆ There has been a census in Britain once every ten years from 1801 to the present *except* in 1941 when the country was at war.

◆ The population of Manchester fell by almost 120 000 (about 18 per cent) in just ten years after 1961. This was the peak period for slum clearance in the inner city.

ocus Points 1 and 2

◆ Give two **push factors** that made people want to leave inner city areas. Give two **pull factors** that attracted them to suburban housing areas.

◆ In 1981 the average number of people in households in Middlesbrough was:
$$\frac{150\ 000}{54\ 000} = 2.8 \text{ people.}$$
In 2006 it is estimated that the average household size will be
$$\frac{140\ 000}{58\ 300} = ? \text{ people.}$$

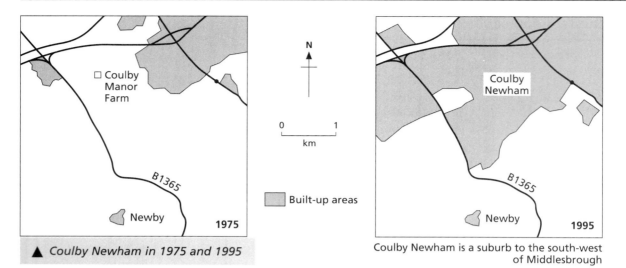

▲ *Coulby Newham in 1975 and 1995*

Coulby Newham is a suburb to the south-west of Middlesbrough

Questions

Development of greenfield sites

Choose a case study of an area on the rural/urban fringe.

1 Describe the new housing estates that have been built on former farmland.

2 Has this new development caused any conflict over land use?

3 Is the development likely to spread in future? Explain your answer.

(c) Changes to the rural environment

In other places small country villages have become 'commuter settlements'. In the past, most people who lived in these villages worked locally, often on farms. Now, many of the houses and other buildings have been bought by people from cities, and converted into luxury houses. Estates of new houses have also been built round the edges of the villages.

For instance, Thurston is a village 14km from Bury St Edmunds in Suffolk. For many years it was an agricultural village with a small market. In 1846 the railway was built to Thurston. The market grew rapidly as produce could be sent more easily to towns and cities. Later, the railway brought commuters who lived in Thurston and worked in Bury St Edmunds. Thurston developed two quite separate sections, a farming village and a commuter village, with the church in between.

From 1950 onwards, as car ownership grew, many more people moved to the village. The gap between the two parts of the village was filled with new estates. Some newcomers worked in Bury St Edmunds, but now some travel to London to work. Meanwhile the number of farm workers in the village declined. This was mainly due to mechanization of work on the land.

A commuter is a person who lives in a village or small town and travels to work in another town or city.

Note Some geographers think commuting may decline in future, as telecommunications let people work at home and send all their work over the Internet.

At the same time some businesses wanted to move into the village. The old grain store by the station was converted into business units for small companies. Now, the rural nature of Thurston has disappeared almost completely. Most of the village shops have closed. People travel to the superstores on the edge of Bury St Edmunds for most of their shopping.

Thurston was able to grow because it was outside the London 'green belt'. A 'green belt' is an area around a big city where planning controls are very strict. The authorities try to stop new building in green belts, so that the cities will not continue to spread and sprawl across the countryside. Green belts conserve countryside close to cities. However, some people think that the green belt policy should be changed. Green belts do not cut demand for new building land: they just put greater pressure on land near cities that is not protected.

ocus Point 3

Transport changes have brought changes to Thurston village.

How did the railway change:
(a) Thurston's market function
(b) the type of residents in Thurston?

How did the growth of private car ownership affect:
(a) the type of residents
(b) the village shops?

uestions

The effects of counterurbanization

Many issues arise when a lot of newcomers from cities move into rural villages. Some are considered below. Think about these, in your own case study areas, and in Thurston.

1 What should happen when people born in the village cannot afford houses in the village, because town people buy them at high prices?

2 Many village shops have closed in recent years. People blame commuters and second-home owners, increased car ownership, and hypermarkets in cities. Who suffers when the shops close? What can be done to save village shops?

3 Some businesses are moving out of cities to locate in villages. Electronic communications like e-mail and the Internet make this easier. Should such changes be encouraged? Who benefits? Does anyone suffer?

(d) Redevelopment of old inner city areas

Re-read page 21 for an example of how the EU has provided funds to help urban change.

Gateshead is a medium-sized town which is part of the Tyneside conurbation. It lies to the south of the River Tyne, opposite its larger neighbour, Newcastle. In the 1950s it had many urban problems, such as declining industry and large areas of old, crowded, poor-quality 'slum' housing. The council was determined to improve the situation, so it started a programme of urban renewal. This involved clearing the worst of the slums, and rebuilding new housing to replace them. The sketch map on the next page shows some of the phases of redevelopment that have taken place.

A conurbation is found where several towns and/or cities have spread until they merge and form a single, large urban area.

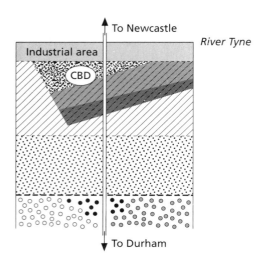

To Newcastle

River Tyne

Industrial area

CBD

To Durham

|| A1 (old Durham Road)

 Mainly middle-class suburban housing

▨▨▨ Mainly old inner city housing

– – – Edge of city

Phase 1   Redevelopment 1960s
Terraced houses cleared. Blocks of flats built. Had all amenities but often damp, lacked privacy, not popular, no sense of community.

Some people moved out from inner city to out-of-town council estates

Phase 2   Redevelopment 1970s
Low-rise but high-density redevelopment. Quite successful when each house had its own private space. Less successful when there was a lot of shared communal space.

Rapid growth of out-of-town council estates

Phase 3   Redevelopment 1980s
Conservative Government cut funds for council housing. Encouraged housing associations. Small-scale redevelopment of estates for rent. More renovation rather than demolition – new kitchens, bathrooms, damp-proofing, etc.

Much growth of private housing

▲ *Redevelopment of old inner city areas*

Questions

Redevelopment of old inner city areas

1 Name a case study area where attempts have been made to improve housing near the centre of a town or city.

2 Describe the problems before the improvement started.

3 What was done to try to improve conditions?

4 Can you identify 'phases' where different solutions were tried, as in Gateshead?

5 In what ways has the redevelopment been successful? Who has benefited?

6 Have any problems been caused by the redevelopment? Who has suffered?

7 In your opinion, what still needs to be done? Will the area improve in future?

(e) Changes in the location and character of shopping centres

Out-of-town shopping centres versus CBDs
The map opposite was in a geography textbook published in 1979. It was a popular book, up to date with the latest geography at that time. It shows four different types and sizes of retail outlets, but it does *not*

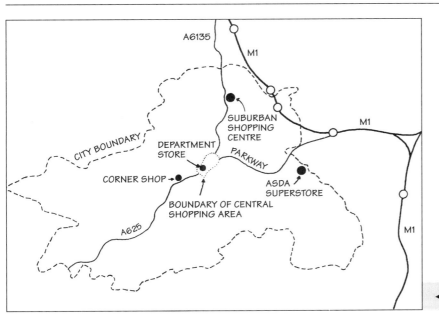

◀ *Shopping in the late 1970s*

show any out-of-town shopping centres. If the author had written a new edition of the book after about 1985, such a centre would almost certainly have been included.

The growth of out-of-town shopping has been very important during the 20 years or so since that book was written. They include Lakeside (Thurrock), White Rose Centre (Leeds), Meadowhall (Sheffield – the city shown on the map above) and Merry Hill Centre in Dudley. What are the advantages of these centres that have caused their rapid growth?

Advantages
- Land is cheaper on the edge of cities than in the CBDs.

- There is plenty of space for car parking. Stores that need a very large floor area have enough space to build on one level.

- New buildings can be put up without the costs of demolishing old ones, or fitting them around existing buildings.

- Because they are new they can build in all the latest ideas, and so they have a very modern image.

- They are easily accessible by road, often being close to ring roads, by-passes and motorway interchanges.

The growth of out-of-town shopping produced a lot of competition for CBDs. In order to attract customers, many new developments were introduced into CBDs. These included:

- pedestrian streets, to make shopping pleasanter and safer

- new pick-up points where shoppers could bring their cars close to the stores

- covered arcades to protect shoppers from the weather.

The retail revolution of the 1980s and 1990s has been based on the growth of road transport.

ocus Point 4

Cover the page. List four reasons for the growth of out-of-town shopping centres.

Disadvantages

However, by about 1995, the out-of-town centres were falling out of favour with some people and organizations. What were the reasons for this change?

- Growth of new centres was using up a lot of countryside, threatening areas of green belt.

- Shops in city centres were threatened by the competition from out-of-town centres.

- The new centres were only really accessible by car. This made it difficult for people without cars (the young, old, disabled, poor, single-parent families, etc.) to use them.

- They encourage increased use of cars, causing extra congestion, pollution, etc.

As a result of these problems, politicians and planners are bringing in stricter rules to make it more difficult to develop out-of-town shopping centres.

ocus Point 5

Cover the page. List four problems caused by the growth of out-of-town shopping centres.

Questions

Shopping centres

1 Name one example of an out-of-town shopping centre that you have studied.

2 Draw a sketch map to show its location.

3 Label the sketch map to show why this was a good place to build.

4 Describe the market area of the centre. Either do this in words, or draw a map to show the area served by the development.

5 Has the growth of this centre affected trade in the CBD of the local town?

6 Has the CBD been altered to try to compete with the out-of-town centre?

Superstores versus small shops

The map on page 31 does show a superstore on the edge of the city. These began to appear in the United Kingdom in the 1970s, and have grown in size and importance ever since. Now, in the late 1990s, four chainstores dominate the market for the weekly household shopping: Tesco, Sainsburys, Asda and Safeway.

All these companies build big stores close to major roads, positioned to attract people from a radius of up to about 24km (15 miles). This is less than the out-of-town centres, which aim to attract people from a much larger area. As they are so big the superstores sell a very large volume of goods. They can offer low prices, and still make good profits because of this big turnover.

As time has passed the superstores have started to offer a bigger and bigger range of goods. This is very convenient for their customers, because they can buy lots of different things at the same time. However, the growth of the superstores has put many small shops out of business, and threatens many others. For instance:

Superstores sell:	This threatens the future of:
fresh vegetables	greengrocers and market stalls
fresh bread	bakers
newspapers	newsagents
beer and wine	off-licences
medicines	chemists
etc.	etc.

Of course, most customers welcome the low prices and convenience, but as the superstores grow, corner shops, high street shops, suburban shopping parades, village stores and many other services are disappearing. Then what happens to the people who cannot afford cars and cannot get to the superstores? Once again, the poor and the less mobile lose out.

Questions

Superstores

1 Name a local superstore.

2 Describe its market area.

3 From your own knowledge, or by interviewing people who have known the area for longer than you, name any shops that have closed since the opening of the superstore.

Growth of market areas

People are becoming more mobile as car ownership increases and as some forms of public transport increase. The growth of superstores and out-of-town shopping centres illustrates this. Both of these types of retail outlet need to have a very large market area in order to survive.

Some shopping centres are even developing international market areas. Cross-Channel travel has become so cheap that many shoppers travel across the Channel to shop.

British people go to France for:	French people come to England for:
• wine and beer, which is cheaper because lower rates of tax	• 'speciality goods' like marmalade and Earl Grey tea
• 'speciality goods' like cheeses	• to buy 'typically English' brands of clothes, such as Marks and Spencer and Barbour jackets
• designer-label clothes	

Focus Point 6

Some superstores are also starting to offer savings accounts, insurance sales, and even money loans. How will this affect businesses in the high street?

People who go on long-distance shopping trips may be able to save money, but only people who are fairly well off can afford the cost of the fares in the first place.

Exam practice

Since the Second World War there have been many changes in the types of transport people use, and in the cost of transport. These changes have led to big changes in the structure of cities and rural settlements. Choose any two of the changes listed below:

(a) the movement of people from inner cities out to the suburbs, and beyond

(b) changes to the areas where towns and cities meet the countryside

(c) changes to the rural environment

(d) redevelopment of old inner city areas

(e) changes in the location and character of shopping centres.

Explain why changes in transport have led to **each** of the changes you have chosen. Make detailed reference to one or more areas that you have studied.   (20 lines 10 marks)

2 Managing natural environments

A i) Managing landscape systems

> **Key idea 1**   **Scale**
>
> Natural environments are systems, consisting of inputs, processes and outputs.   *Local*
> These systems interact with people.   *International*
>
> **Expanded key idea**
> The idea of a **system** is a useful way of organizing information in geography. A system is part of the world that we have to study. It is connected to the rest of the world but, for the purpose of our study, it is useful to see it simply and separately. We need to look at the **processes** that go on in the system. These can often be described as **flows** or **transfers of energy**. Energy can also be **stored** in the system. All the systems studied in geography also have **inputs** coming from the rest of the world, and **outputs** going back into the world.

A system model

In another part of this syllabus we study drainage basin systems as part of the water cycle. Here we will look at the tropical rainforest ecosystem.

The tropical rainforest ecosystem

Inputs
The main **inputs** are:

- minerals from the soil

- heat + light from the sun   temperature is high all year – so plants can grow

- moisture from rainfall   rain falls all year round, for 12 months of the year.

Focus Point 1

Link the words in column A with words in column B for a drainage basin:

A	B
Input	Erosion
Process	Evapotrans-piration
Transfer	Lake
Storage	Rainfall
Output	Run-off

Stores
The main **stores** in the system are:

in the soil
- minerals from weathered rock
- humus from decayed plant and animal material
- water

in the vegetation
- minerals and nutrients are used to form plant matter – also known as **biomass**

on the ground
- dead and decaying plant matter – also known as **litter**.

In the rainforest ecosystem there is usually a much larger percentage of energy and nutrients stored in the vegetation than in the soil or on the ground. This is because the decay of dead matter, and the take-up of nutrients by the plants, is very fast in the hot, humid environment.

Flows
Flows constantly transfer matter and energy from soil to vegetation to the litter layer and back into the soil. These flows include:

- dead leaves falling to the ground

- decayed leaf material being carried into the soil by worms.

Processes
Some important **processes** are:

• Photosynthesis	Green plants use minerals and water to produce new plant material. This needs sunlight.	Plants compete to grow up to reach the light.	Tall trunks, canopy, lianas
• Decay of plant debris	Leaves, dead wood etc. fall to the forest floor. They decay quickly in the hot, moist conditions.	This produces plant nutrients, which are used almost straight away for rapid plant growth.	Thin soils, shallow roots, buttress roots to support trees.

Outputs
When rainforest is left in its natural state, there are very few **outputs**:

- Water that has been used by plants is lost from leaf surfaces by evapotranspiration.

- Some water runs into rivers as throughflow or overland flow.

- Water running through the soil leaches some minerals out of the soil.

◆ The main thing that limits growth of new plants is shortage of sunlight. The thick canopy cuts out about 80 per cent of sunlight and makes the forest floor a very shady place.

◆ Rainforests have very luxuriant vegetation but soils are usually very poor. This is because most of the nutrients are taken up by fast-growing plants.

ocus Point 2

Explain why rainforest trees often have tall, straight trunks and buttress roots.

The word 'buttress' was originally used in architecture to describe a supporting wall in a cathedral or castle. The buttress was built at right-angles to the main wall to strengthen it.

However, when human activity alters the natural ecosystem, changes to the outputs can take place. For example:

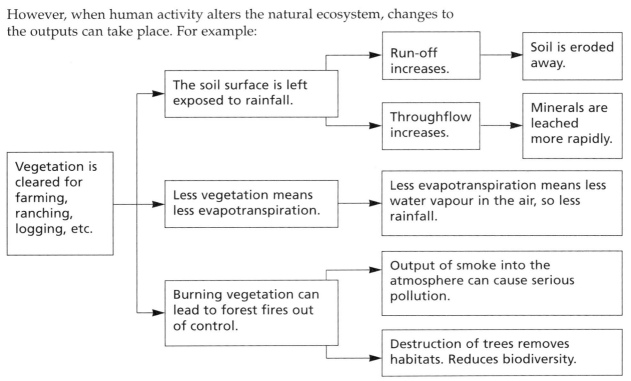

Vegetation is cleared for farming, ranching, logging, etc.	**The soil surface is left exposed to rainfall.** → **Run-off increases.** → **Soil is eroded away.** → **Throughflow increases.** → **Minerals are leached more rapidly.**
	Less vegetation means less evapotranspiration. → **Less evapotranspiration means less water vapour in the air, so less rainfall.**
	Burning vegetation can lead to forest fires out of control. → **Output of smoke into the atmosphere can cause serious pollution.** → **Destruction of trees removes habitats. Reduces biodiversity.**

Human influences on the rainforest ecosystem

People have always made use of rainforests. For hundreds and even thousands of years they have used the land for farming and mining, they have used the trees for fruit, nuts, medicines, building wood, firewood and even for magic rituals, and they have hunted and domesticated animals and birds. However, in the past 40 years or so the rate of use has increased, and the area that has been seriously affected by over-use has grown rapidly.

Sustainable development means:

- encouraging development so that people can have an improved standard of living

- making sure that the environment is not destroyed, so that the improved standard of living will continue. Many human activities can be sustainable, if they are well managed; but if they are badly managed they can destroy the ecosystem. Some examples are given in the table on the next page.

◆ Destruction of the rainforest is a serious concern in some areas. However, Europeans and Americans are rather hypocritical when they make a big fuss about Brazilians and Africans damaging the precious forest, when most European and North American forests were totally destroyed centuries ago.

	More sustainable	**Less sustainable**
Shifting cultivation	Groups of people use the land to grow crops. Patches of forest are cleared; crops are grown; soil fertility declines; the patch is abandoned and left to recover; the group move on to a new patch of land.	The population of some groups of shifting farmers has grown as health care has been improved. Other groups have lost some of their traditional land to outsiders. In both cases they have to use land more intensively. This takes more out of the soil, so it has less time to recover.
Timber	Trees have always been cut by local people to use for building and fuelwood. They just cut the trees they needed and left the rest of the forest unchanged. Some commercial timber companies (e.g. in Thailand) replant trees in areas they have cleared. They plant species that will be useful in the future. This reduces biodiversity, but does maintain forest cover.	Logging companies use large machines to cut roads through the forest, and then to cut the trees they need. They often clear unwanted trees to allow access to the few valuable trees. Unwanted trees and plants are burnt. This leads to whole areas being cleared of vegetation.
Commercial farming	Plantations for rubber in Malaysia and palms in West Africa have been developed to conserve the soil by making sure that there is always some plant cover to reduce the rate of leaching. They also employ local labour, providing training and good working conditions.	In parts of Amazonia large firms have cleared enormous areas of forest for cattle ranching. The natural vegetation is burnt; grass is planted; cattle graze the area for a few years; then the soil is exhausted and the land is abandoned. The forest does not grow back because such large areas have been cleared that seeds can only spread back into the area very slowly. Also, soil is often very badly eroded.
Mining	Mining can never be truly sustainable. It uses up resources. But in the Carajas region of Brazil the mining company aims to mine iron ore without damaging the forest around the mine. The whole mine area is strictly controlled to stop squatter settlements developing around the mine and the town where workers live.	In many parts of Amazonia, mining of iron ore, gold, etc. has caused great damage. Native inhabitants have been killed or removed; forest has been totally destroyed, both for the mines and for towns, roads and railways. Then large numbers of squatters have moved into the area. They hope to make money growing food for the miners, or looking for casual work at the mines. They cause deforestation to spread out from the original mining area.

 **Questions**

The rainforest

Refer to your rainforest case study. Find examples that illustrate the ideas in this chapter.

 **Focus Point 3**

Describe how subsistence farming, commercial farming, forestry and mining can be made either more or less sustainable.

Exam practice

Clearing rainforest causes (a) exposed soil (b) reduced evapotranspiration (c) forest fires.
Describe how each of these can cause problems for people and the environment.   (15 lines 9 marks)

Landscape: inputs and outputs

> ## Key idea 2
> **Scale**
> A landscape is the product of a system of inputs and processes. These interact *Local*
> to produce distinctive landscapes, including those of great scenic attraction. *Regional*
>
> ### Expanded key idea
> The **inputs** into a landscape include:
> - the rock, which varies in structure, strength, resistance to erosion, etc.
> - the climate of the area
> - people, who can have an enormous effect on landscape.
>
> The **processes** that cause change and development of the landscape include weathering, erosion, deposition and human activity.
>
> Climate has been very different in the past, and so have human influences. It is important to study how past processes have influenced present-day landscapes.

Glaciated uplands in Britain

The Ice Age in Britain lasted from about one million years BP (before the present) to about 20 000 BP. During this time there were several glacial periods, when temperatures fell and ice covered large parts of Britain, separated by interglacial periods. In fact, at the moment we may just be in a warm interglacial before the next glacial period starts, and the ice advances again.

During a glacial period the temperature falls by 5 or 6 °C. This means that more snow falls during the winter. In the highlands it does not all melt during the summer. Gradually the snow builds up and covers larger and larger areas with permanent snowfields. Snow is made up of ice crystals, separated by large volumes of air. But as the thickness of the snow cover increases, the lower layers are compressed by the weight above. This squeezes the air out and turns the snow into ice. This ice is much more dense and harder than snow.

In some areas, after several decades of build-up of snow and ice, the weight can force the lower layers to start to move and flow outwards from the centre of accumulation. In highland areas the flowing ice moves downhill, following the valleys. These 'rivers of ice' are called **glaciers**.

Erosion by ice

Before glaciers form there is usually a period of very cold weather when the rocks are weakened by freeze–thaw weathering. This can weaken or even shatter the rocks. Moving ice can erode these rocks in two main ways – plucking and abrasion.

DID YOU KNOW? Ben Nevis is the highest mountain in Britain (1045 metres). It is estimated that if it were just 50 metres higher it could be cold enough there to have snow all through the year.

Note Imagine making a snowball. You take soft snow and squeeze it to make it firmer. By compressing it you squeeze out the air, and the ice crystals become more compact. This is similar to what happens when snow turns to ice in a glacier.

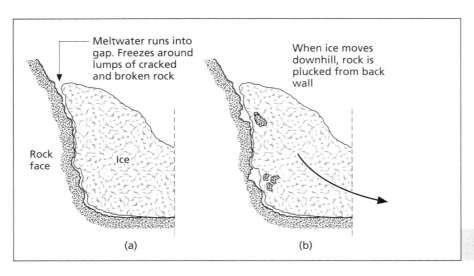

Meltwater runs into gap. Freezes around lumps of cracked and broken rock

Rock face

Ice

(a)

When ice moves downhill, rock is plucked from back wall

(b)

◀ *Plucking*

When water freezes to form ice, its volume increases by about 10 per cent. If water is trapped in cracks in rock this can put great pressure on the rock. After repeated freezing and thawing the rock may finally crack.

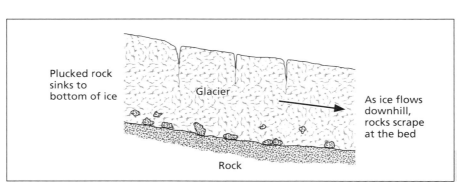

Plucked rock sinks to bottom of ice

Glacier

As ice flows downhill, rocks scrape at the bed

Rock

◀ *Abrasion*

Focus **Point 1**

Cover up the diagrams. Practise drawing them. Now describe how plucking and abrasion happen.

These processes of weathering and erosion form features such as:

- **Corries** (called **cwms** in Wales and **cirques** in France) are deep hollows on a mountainside. They have very steep back walls which are often partly covered by scree (small loose rocks). They have rounded or flat bottoms, which may contain small lakes or tarns. There is often a rocky lip, where the glacier flowed out of the corrie.

Hints and Tips!

Some people describe corries as 'deep, armchair-shaped hollows'. If this phrase helps you to visualize a corrie, then remember it!

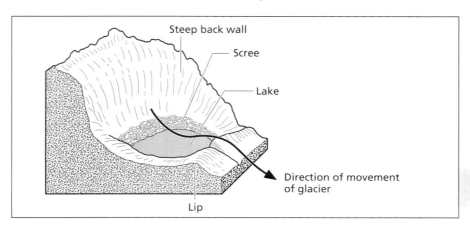

Steep back wall

Scree

Lake

Direction of movement of glacier

Lip

◀ *Cross-section of a corrie*

- **Arêtes** (or **knife-edge ridges**) are steep-sided ridges of land between two corries. The sides may fall for hundreds of metres, and the tops may be only one or two metres across.

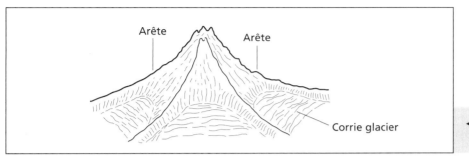

◀ *Arêtes between a group of corries*

- **Glacial troughs** (or **U-shaped valleys**) are steep-sided, flat-bottomed valleys. They are usually fairly straight, because the glaciers that eroded them flowed straight, unlike rivers which meander. Some glacial troughs have long, narrow **finger lakes** in them.

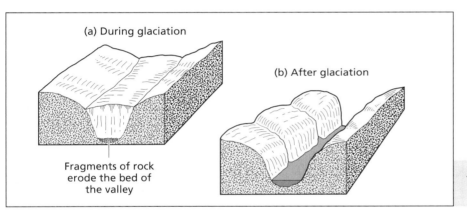

◀ *U-shaped valley or glaciated trough*

 **ocus Point 2**

Choose *either* a corrie *or* an arête *or* a U-shaped valley. Explain how plucking and abrasion helped to form your chosen feature.

Questions

Corries, arêtes and glacial troughs

Learn the names of examples of the features listed above. You should be able to locate them on a map, and describe them.

The attractions of glaciated landscapes

- Most of the areas where glaciation starts are highlands. This is because temperatures are lower in highlands.

- Highlands are also usually areas of hard rock because hard rock is resistant to erosion. Soft rocks get worn down to form lowlands.

- Glaciers are, therefore, mainly found in areas of high land, with hard rock, and this means they produce spectacular scenery.

The valleys were made deep by the ice, but the land in between the valleys now forms high peaks. The soil was scraped away from the high land by the ice, leaving the rock exposed, but even this rock is cracked and broken by ice. It forms steep cliffs and jagged ridges, with spectacular waterfalls flowing from them, down to the flat green valleys in between.

The land in glaciated areas is wild and spectacular, and it attracts many people for outdoor leisure. Some come just to admire the scenery, but it also attracts walkers, rock climbers, skiers, hang glider pilots, canoeists, mountain bikers, bird watchers, campers, and many others.

Unfortunately, so many people may come to this wild, unspoilt scenery that it may start to be damaged and spoilt.

Limestone scenery in National Parks in England and Wales

National Parks were first set up in England and Wales with two aims:

- to protect areas of beautiful, unspoilt scenery from development

- to encourage people to use this land for leisure pursuits.

Most of the National Parks are in highland areas. In some, like the Lake District and Snowdonia, the scenery is largely a result of erosion by valley glaciers. In others the presence of limestone rock has been a very big influence.

Limestone is an **organic, sedimentary rock**. That means it was formed from the remains of marine creatures deposited on the sea bed. They were compressed to form solid rock.

Limestone produces a very special type of landscape, sometimes called **karst scenery**. It is a result of weathering of the rock. The type and speed of weathering is largely a result of the chemistry and structure of limestone.

Hints and Tips!

◆ You may be asked to give examples of how glaciated scenery is used for outdoor pursuits. Try to be precise. An answer that says 'Glaciated scenery can be used for walking' will gain some credit. One that says 'Glaciated scenery, like the Bwlch Main arête on the side of Snowdon, can be used for walking' will gain more marks.

◆ The two reasons for setting up National Parks should be easy to learn. So learn them exactly!

Focus Point 3

What is the meaning of 'organic' and 'sedimentary' when they are used to describe a rock such as limestone? Make sure you know the definitions of both words.

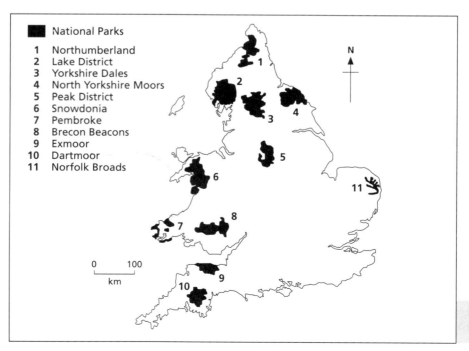

National Parks

1 Northumberland
2 Lake District
3 Yorkshire Dales
4 North Yorkshire Moors
5 Peak District
6 Snowdonia
7 Pembroke
8 Brecon Beacons
9 Exmoor
10 Dartmoor
11 Norfolk Broads

0   100
km

◀ National Parks in England and Wales

The chemistry of limestone

The type of limestone that is found in the Yorkshire Dales and Peak District Parks is called Carboniferous limestone. It is fairly hard so it is quite resistant to erosion. However, it is soluble. It can be weathered by the chemical action of rainwater which dissolves the rock. Rainwater contains some carbon dioxide, picked up as the rain falls through the atmosphere. The chemistry of this reaction is:

Calcium carbonate	+	Water	+	Carbon dioxide	=	Calcium bicarbonate
$CaCO_3$		H_2O		CO_2		$Ca(HCO_3)_2$

Calcium bicarbonate can be carried away in solution.

The structure of limestone

Carboniferous limestone was formed in layers, or **strata**, on the sea bed. These layers are separated by cracks, parallel to each other, called **bedding planes**. At right-angles to the bedding planes are more cracks, called **joints**. These divide the rock up into a series of blocks. The size of the blocks varies, but they are often about 0.5 to 2 metres square, and about one metre deep.

The joints and bedding planes make the rock **permeable**. Water can sink into the rock through these lines of weakness. As the water flows through the joints and bedding planes it dissolves some of the rock. This slowly widens the joints, and can produce the following features on the surface, and below ground.

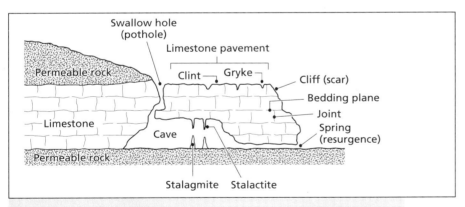

▲ *Cross-section through limestone rock showing major features*

The exposed rock surface that forms limestone pavements is probably due to two factors.

- Any soil that had formed on the rock was carried away by moving ice during the Ice Age.

- Since the end of the Ice Age, new soil has not formed, because most weathered rock is carried away in solution. This means that vegetation cannot grow, and soil cannot form.

ocus Point 4

Cover up the page. Write out the equation for weathering of limestone. Use either words or chemical formulae.

Hints and Tips!

◆ To remember the difference between clints and grykes: **g**rykes are like **g**rooves in the rock.

◆ Just in case you do not know this already, remember that stala**c**tites hang from the **c**eiling of the cave, and stala**g**mites grow on the **g**round.

Limestone and leisure

Weathered limestone produces a very attractive landscape. The steep slopes and thin soils mean that the land has been used mainly for grazing animals, especially sheep, and not often for arable farming. This has left the land ideal for walking, rock climbing and many other outdoor pursuits. Another special attraction is the network of underground caves which are ideal for potholers to explore.

There are often land use conflicts in the limestone regions. These develop from the problems of meeting the needs of tourists and those of the farmers, quarrymen, naturalists and others who make their living from the land.

Questions

Limestone scenery

Refer to a case study area in a limestone National Park.

1 Describe an example of land use conflict.

2 Explain how both sides wish to use the land.

3 Can the conflict be resolved by careful planning?

Focus Point 5

Draw a quick sketch of a limestone pavement, and label: bedding plane, joint, clint, gryke.

Potholing is very dangerous for inexperienced people. This is partly because water can flow very quickly through the joints and bedding planes of the permeable rock. So when it rains, underground streams can rise very quickly and flood the cave systems.

A ii) Managing drainage basin systems

Key ideas 3–6	Scale
Drainage basins are systems which are part of the hydrological cycle. They must be managed carefully, as changes in one part of the system can affect all other parts of the system.	*Local* *Regional* *International*

Expanded key idea

A drainage basin system has inputs, transfers, stores and outputs (see page 35). These can be influenced by physical and human activities. The water in drainage basins has many uses, but drainage basins must be managed carefully, because all parts of the system are interconnected. Changes to one part of the system can have great effects on other parts of the system. These are often unexpected.

River systems in the hydrological cycle

The hydrological cycle (or water cycle) shows how water is transferred from the sea to the land, then back again to the sea. Diagrams showing the cycle are very simplified. They often show all the water that falls as precipitation onto the land flowing back to the sea, over the surface, as run-off. The full picture is far more complicated, as a study of drainage basins shows.

However, it is important to understand the basic features of the hydrological cycle. Energy from the sun evaporates water. This evaporation can happen over land as well as over the sea. Water vapour is then carried over the land, by winds. Here the air may be cooled, causing condensation, then precipitation.

Focus Point 1

Cover the page. Draw a labelled diagram showing evaporation, condensation, precipitation and run-off in the water cycle. Learn this precisely.

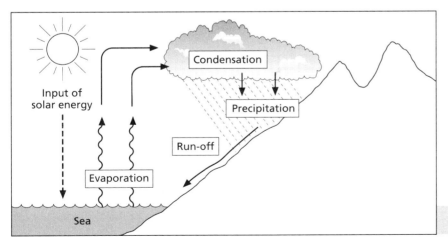

◀ *The hydrological cycle*

The movement of water through a drainage basin

Water is an input into the drainage basin in the form of **precipitation**. This can be rainfall, snow, sleet, hail, dew or frost. Then the water can pass through several types of **transfer**, or be kept in several different **stores**.

Transfers	Stores
• Unchannelled surface flow • Channelled flow in rivers • Soil throughflow • Groundwater flow • Take-up by plants • Evaporation* • Evapotranspiration*	• Snowfields or icecaps • Lakes, ponds, puddles, etc. • Soil moisture storage • Groundwater storage (in permeable rocks) • Storage as plant moisture

* these two transfers take water out of the river system

The transfers and stores listed in the table are all natural processes. People can store water in reservoirs, tanks, etc. and transfer it along pipes, channels, etc.

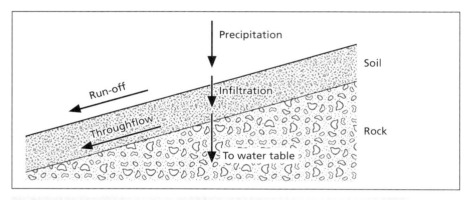

Precipitation

Soil

Run-off

Infiltration

Throughflow

Rock

To water table

▲ *What happens to precipitation when it reaches the surface?*

Exactly which route water takes through the river system depends on many interrelated factors. These include:

- **Intensity of the rainfall** – during light rainfall much of the water soaks into the ground. When rain is heavier it may not all infiltrate (soak through), so run-off increases.

- **Length of rainfall period** – if there has been a long period of rainfall the ground may be saturated (waterlogged). If there is any more rain it will lead to surface run-off.

- **Nature of the rock** – if the rock is permeable (e.g. limestone), water can soak into it, and be stored as groundwater. Impermeable rock (such as shale) will not let water soak in, and this also increases run-off.

- **Vegetation cover** – the leaves of plants intercept the rainfall. This can slow it down, so it does not run off as quickly. Plant roots help to break up the soil, and allow water to infiltrate more easily, and this also reduces run-off.

- **Soil depth and structure** – a deep soil can hold more water, storing it and reducing the speed at which it reaches the river. A good soil has plenty of humus, and this also helps to absorb water.

All rain is caused by air rising and cooling, leading to condensation. The air can be forced to rise in three different ways: by convection, by relief, or at a front.

ocus Point 2

Cover the page, then list three natural transfers, three natural stores, two human transfers and two human stores that are all part of the hydrological cycle.

Note
Remember, the faster rainwater gets to the stream, the more likely it is to cause a flood.

- **Building and farming** – when the surface is built over with houses or tarmac, water cannot infiltrate. This increases the rate of run-off. Overgrazing by animals can compact the soil, and makes infiltration difficult. The weight of heavy machinery on the land can also do this.

What is a drainage basin?

A river is a channel of running water. It is fed by water that runs into it, often from a very wide area. Some water reaches the main river through smaller rivers or **tributaries**. These join the main stream at **confluences**.

Any water that falls onto the surface in between the river and its tributaries runs towards one of the streams. It may flow over the surface (as **run-off**) or it may flow through the soil (as **throughflow**), but it flows down the slope of the land. At the bottom of slopes there is usually a stream, flowing in a **valley**.

The whole area that is drained by a river and its tributaries is called a **drainage basin**. Basins are usually surrounded by higher land – except at the mouth. The highest land, which separates one river basin from the next, is called the **watershed**.

This map shows the drainage basin of the Ganges river system. To the north lie the Himalayas and to the south is the Deccan Plateau. The river flows into the Bay of Bengal, through its delta. Here the river splits up into smaller channels, called **distributaries**.

ocus Point 3

Would these actions make a flood more likely or less likely?
(a) Cutting down an area of woodland and ploughing the soil.
(b) Putting drains into an area of marshland, so that it can be used for arable crops.
(c) Reducing the size of a flock of sheep, to stop them over-grazing the land.
(d) Building a new housing estate on a hillside.

ocus Point 4

Cover the page. Now give one word for each of these definitions:
(a) A small river that joins a larger river.
(b) Water that flows over the surface of the land.
(c) The line that marks the edge of a river basin.
(d) A small stream that takes some water from the main river across a delta.

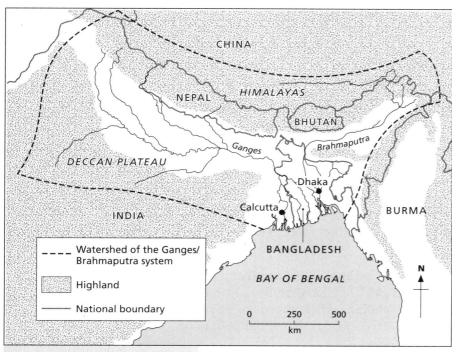

▲ *The Ganges drainage basin*

Case Study

Flooding in the Ganges basin – physical factors

The Ganges basin lies in the region of monsoon climate. This means that the seasonal pattern of rainfall is very uneven.

Rainfall is concentrated in the period between April and September, and so the rivers regularly flood after the heavy rainfall. Many farmers rely on the floods to provide both water for the crops, and sediment (earth loosened by the flood waters) to fertilize the fields. In the dry season from November to March, rivers fall to very low levels.

Another aspect of the region's climate can also cause flooding. In late summer and autumn, tropical cyclones form over the Bay of Bengal. They blow in towards the coast of India and Bangladesh. They bring heavy rain and tidal surges, which both increase the flood risk in the lower valley and the delta.

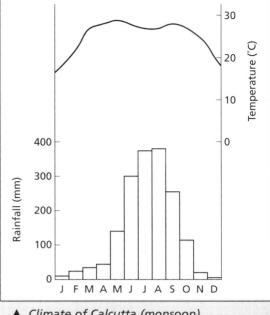

▲ *Climate of Calcutta (monsoon)*

Flooding in the Ganges basin – human factors

In this section it is important to ask three questions about the interrelationship between the rivers and the people:

1 Are human activities increasing the number and intensity of floods?
In many parts of the catchment area of the Ganges, deforestation is taking place. People clear trees for farmland, and to provide fuelwood and building material. It seems certain that this has led to increased flooding in parts of Nepal and Bhutan, close to where the clearance has taken place. This is a result of:

- less **interception** of rainfall by plant leaves

- less **infiltration** of water into the soil, because land that is not protected by vegetation gets baked hard by the sun

- less **take-up** of water by plant roots

- more **erosion** of soil, because it is no longer bound together by plant roots. This leads to sediment being deposited on the floodplains, blocking rivers.

In addition there has probably been an increase in the number of severe cyclones coming from the Bay of Bengal. They have caused greater damage and loss of life, because population growth means more people are now forced to live on the floodplains, in areas that are known to be particularly dangerous during a cyclone.

2 How important are the floods to the people who live near to the rivers?
The regular, annual flooding is absolutely vital to the people who live on the delta and floodplain of these rivers. People have adapted their

Note When the monsoon causes the Ganges to flood, the water usually rises slowly and predictably. People can prepare for the flood. Tropical storms are usually sudden and far less predictable. Therefore the floods they bring can cause far more damage.

 **ocus Point 5**

Give three reasons why deforestation can increase flooding downstream.

Give one piece of evidence which suggests that deforestation in the Himalayas has *not* caused increased flooding on the Ganges floodplain.

lives to the floods. Most people live on higher mounds of land, above the normal flood level. The roads and tracks are also built along natural or artificial banks.

The farming season is planned around the floods. Rice is the main crop and there are many different varieties. Each is adapted to slight differences in temperature, length of growing season, and depth of the floodwater in the fields. The various types are planted in different areas as the floodwaters advance and then retreat. Without the floods the very high population densities in this area could not be supported by the land.

Seasonally flooded land also provides feeding grounds for many freshwater fish. They provide a vital food source for the inhabitants. For many poor people these fish are their main source of protein.

3 What is being done, and what more could be done, to reduce the damaging effects of the floods?

Some floods do cause great damage. After the 1988 floods, the Bangladesh government and international aid donors set up the **Flood Action Plan (FAP)**. To try to control river flooding, banks are being built, or strengthened, along most of the major rivers across the delta and the floodplain. These have to allow 'controlled flooding'. Sluice gates let 'normal' floodwater onto the land to irrigate it, but keep the excess water in the rivers.

In some areas the FAP is trying to encourage people to move further away from the river during the flood season. They will only do this if they can grow their crops during the dry season, so the FAP is trying to provide more irrigation water during the dry period.

Other FAP projects include:

- improving flood warning systems

- providing shelters on raised legs, which can protect large numbers of people from both river floods and seawater floods, caused by cyclones (see page 72)

- raising the mounds that homes are built on.

In other words, the FAP is trying to help and encourage Bangladeshi people to 'live with the floods'.

Questions

Drainage basins

Give examples to show how drainage basins are managed to provide water supply. Include examples of:
- local scale, to show how water is provided for domestic use
- regional or international scale, to show how a multiple-purpose scheme manages a major river basin such as the Colorado or Nile, so that it can be used for irrigation, HEP, navigation, etc.

Some people fear that the spread of high-yielding varieties of rice (HYVs), produced by genetic engineering, could result in some of the specialized local varieties being abandoned.

Note Only people with detailed local knowledge can plan properly to make sure that the FAP meets local needs. As with many projects in LEDCs, outsiders can give useful advice – but they must not ignore local knowledge and just tell people what is best for them.

Focus Point 6

Cover the page. Give four examples of ways in which the FAP is helping local people to 'live with the floods'.

B i) People and ecosystems

Key idea 1	Scale

Key idea 1

Farming is a system with inputs, processes and outputs.

Scale
Local
Regional
Global

Expanded key idea

The process of farming is complex, but it can be understood by looking at the **inputs**, including natural inputs and human inputs; the **processes**, or what happens on the farm; and the **outputs**, or the things that are produced and either sold or consumed on the farm.

Classification of farms

The natural environment – soil, climate, slope and relief – has a big effect on what can be grown on any farm. It allows some crops to be grown, but makes it impossible to grow others. For instance, in East Anglia wheat, grass, barley, and sugar beet will all grow, but bananas will not, because the temperature is too low.

The farmer can choose what to grow, within limits. What he chooses depends on his knowledge, skills and interests and also on the prices he can get for each crop at the market. He is also influenced by government policies which make some crops more attractive by paying subsidies, and make others less attractive by putting quotas (or limits) on the amount that can be grown.

It is very useful for geographers to be able to classify farms into different groups. It makes studying farming easier if we identify the key features of different farming systems. All farms can be classified in three ways. These put farms in groups depending on their inputs, processes and outputs.

Classification by inputs

Hints and Tips!

These classifications make good plans for exam answers. For instance:

I have to write about different types of farming. First I will describe intensive farming. Then I will look at differences between capital and labour intensive. Finally I will write about extensive farming.

INTENSIVE FARMING	Examples
These farms have large amounts of inputs on a comparatively small area of land. They are usually found on good land. Money and time invested in such land will bring good profits for the farmer.	
Capital intensive Invests a lot of money in machinery, seeds, fertilizers, irrigation, etc.	• Cereal farming in East Anglia
Labour intensive Puts a lot of work into a small area of land.	• Rice farming on the Ganges floodplain
Capital and labour intensive Invests a lot of money, and uses a lot of labour.	• Greenhouse cultivation of tomatoes in the Netherlands • Small dairy farm in Cheshire

EXTENSIVE FARMING	Examples
These farms have comparatively small inputs for large areas of land. They are usually found where conditions are poor, so it is not a worth farmers putting a lot of money or work into the land.	• Hill sheep farming in upland Britain • Cattle ranching on the dry prairies of the USA

Classification by processes

	Examples
Arable Grows crops, mainly cereals such as rice, wheat, barley, maize (or corn) and millet.	• Crop farming in East Anglia • Rice growing on the Ganges floodplain
Pastoral Keeps animals for meat, milk, skins, wool, etc.	• Hill sheep farming in upland Britain • Cattle ranching in the USA
Market gardening Grows fruit, flowers or vegetables.	• Growing tomatoes in the Netherlands
Mixed Usually combines arable farming with keeping some animals.	• Dairy farming in Cheshire

Classification by outputs

	Examples
Commercial The outputs from the farm are mainly or entirely for sale.	• Arable farming in East Anglia • Ranching in the USA
Subsistence The outputs of the farm are eaten or used by the family who run the farm. In good years there may be some produce left over for sale.	• Rice growing on the Ganges floodplain • Shifting cultivation in Amazonia

Using the full classification
Notice that the same places keep coming up in each list. For instance, cattle ranching in the USA is extensive, and pastoral, and commercial. It can be described in three different ways.

Exam practice

(a) Use three terms to classify each of these farming systems:

    (i)   crop farming in East Anglia

    (ii) rice growing on the Ganges floodplain in Bangladesh

    (iii) growing tomatoes in the Netherlands.

(3 lines 3 marks)

(b) Classify each of the following farming systems:

    (i)   The Maasai in East Africa. They are nomads who travel over large areas of Kenya and Tanzania, seeking pasture and water for their cattle. Their main diet consists of milk and blood from their cattle, although they do sometimes trade their cattle for cereals with nearby farmers.

    (ii) A farmer near Dallas, Texas. He grows crops using expensive irrigation water. All his crops are used as fodder for his cattle, using a mechanized feeding system. He sells the cattle to a chain of beefburger restaurants. I M C

    (iii) A couple who grow fruit and vegetables in greenhouses on a smallholding near Southport in Lancashire. They sell most of their produce in their own shop beside the main road from Southport to Liverpool. E Mi c

(3 lines 3 marks)

The rice-growing system

Rice is probably the world's most important food crop. Between a third and a half of the world's population rely on rice as their staple (main)

Although most of the world's rice is grown in south and south-east Asia, much of the world's export trade comes from the USA, Spain and Italy. This is because Asia's rice is mainly used in the countries where it is grown.

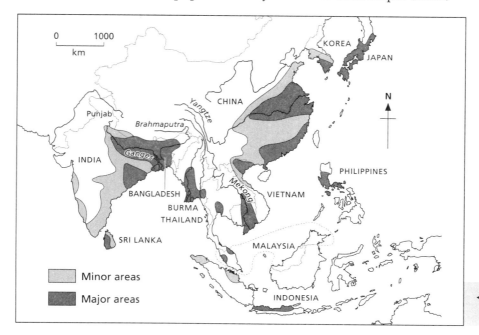

◀ Important rice-growing areas of Asia

food. Rice grows best in the monsoon climates of tropical Asia, and over 80 per cent of the world's production comes from this region. It also grows well in subtropical regions like the Nile valley and southern California, when there is plenty of irrigation water. Some strains of rice even grow in the Mediterranean climate regions of southern Europe.

Ideal rice-growing conditions
Rice grows best with the following natural inputs:

- a growing season of about 5 months, with temperatures above 21°C

- annual rainfall over 2000mm, most falling in the growing season

- a dry spell, after the growing season, for harvesting

- flat land, to allow the water to be kept on the fields

- heavy alluvial soils, to provide nutrients

- impermeable soils, to stop the water draining away from the fields.

The alluvial floodplains of the great rivers of south and east Asia provide these conditions. Temperatures are right, and where rainfall is not high enough the rivers provide irrigation water. The annual floods have also produced soil conditions that are often perfect for growing rice on flooded paddy fields.

Population
These river basins can support very dense populations. Huge areas of China and India have rural population densities over 200/km². These densities are possible because rice can be grown under near-perfect conditions.

However, in the 1950s and 1960s the population of both India and China increased more quickly than it had done in the past. Famine and mass starvation had become a very serious threat in both countries. They realized that if they were to avoid disaster they had to:

- reduce population, or at least slow down the growth

- increase food production.

India and China each brought in policies to deal with the problem. China's population control – the 'one child policy' – received most publicity in the UK. India's main policy was to try and increase food production through the Green Revolution.

The steep volcanic hills of Java have climate and soils that are excellent for rice growing. In order to get the flat land needed, terraces have been cut into the steep slopes. Making and maintaining these terraces is a very labour-intensive process.

 **ocus Point 1**

Cover the page. Give four physical conditions that make an area ideal for rice growing.

Case Study

The Green Revolution in the Punjab

The Punjab (see map on page 52) has always been one of the most productive farming areas in India. The area has good physical conditions for rice growing and a well-trained and educated population. It also has one of the best-developed irrigation systems in India. It was the ideal area to try out the Green Revolution. This involved increasing outputs by increasing inputs.

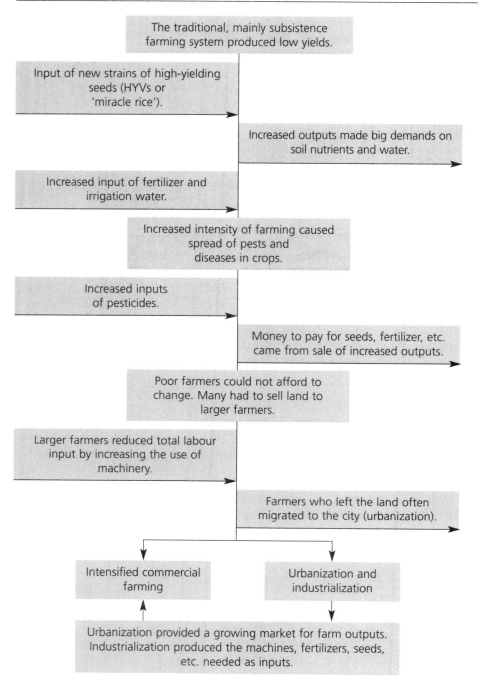

Hints and Tips!

As with many changes, the Green Revolution brought benefits and problems. Make sure that you can write about both in the examination. Aim for balance in your answers.

Focus
Point 2

Name four inputs needed by the Green Revolution. Why did the Green Revolution lead to increased urbanization?

Since the Green Revolution was introduced in the 1960s, there has been a lot of discussion about the advantages and disadvantages of the changes. Many people suffered, because they could not compete with the new, more capital-intensive farmers. They lost their land, and had to adapt to a totally changed way of life. Many moved to the cities, but others stayed in the countryside, working as poor labourers.

However, it is quite clear now that the famines that were predicted did not happen. India has been able to feed its population. Many of the changes that happened in the Punjab in the 1960s have now spread to other parts of India. The ideas have often been spread by education programmes carried on satellite TV, which has been made available in most Indian villages. Farmers have become better educated and more willing to accept new ideas. As this has happened the birth rates are starting to fall in rural areas.

Problems still remain. In particular, there is concern that India's farmers are becoming more dependent on fertilizers, fuel and chemicals made from oil products. This may cause serious long-term problems as these become more scarce but, for now at least, the population is being fed and disaster has been averted.

Not many people realize that India is one of the world's leading countries in terms of use of satellites for TV signals.

Note It is useful to compare China's one child policy with India's slower but less aggressive policy. India's birth rate is falling because people are starting to realize that their living conditions *can* get better, but only if they cut family size.

Farming and the ecosystem

Key idea 2

Farming changes the ecosystem but the effects are more drastic in some areas than in others.

Scale
Local
Regional
International

Expanded key idea

Communities of plants and animals develop in certain areas as a natural response to the climate and soil conditions. As the vegetation develops it affects the development of the soil and, to a lesser extent, the development of the climate. Climate, soil and vegetation together form an ecosystem.

Any attempt to farm an area changes the natural ecosystem. Farmers select certain plants and animals and encourage them to grow. They have to stop other plants and animals from growing. If farmers are not careful they can upset the whole balance of the environment, and can cause drastic changes to the soil and climate.

Soil erosion

It is easy to take soil for granted. People who do not work with soil often think of it as 'dirt'. In fact soil is wonderfully complex and delicate, and is essential for human life. Soil is made up of:

- minerals – fine particles of broken and weathered rock

- humus – a crumbly, black substance, formed from the decomposition of dead plant and animal material

- water – which is held in the soil by the humus

- air – which fills the pore spaces between the mineral particles

- organisms – micro-organisms like bacteria which help break down waste to form humus, and larger creatures like worms, which break up and mix the soil.

Healthy soil has a good 'structure'. Mineral particles and humus become bonded together, and hold moisture. This forms little 'crumbs' that are roughly the size and shape of breadcrumbs. A soil like this contains the nutrients needed for plant growth, and the plants have roots which help bind the soil together. They also recycle organic material, taking it up as they grow, and returning it when they die.

Poor farm management can destroy soil structure. This happens when the farmer takes too much out of the land, without replacing it with inputs, or without recycling humus back into the soil. Then the soil crumb structure is lost and it becomes loose and dusty, and can easily be washed away by water or blown away by wind.

ocus Point 1

Cover the page. List the five components of soil.

Hints and Tips!

Imagine a cycle of nutrients

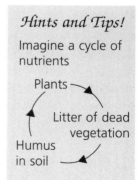

Plants

Litter of dead vegetation

Humus in soil

Poor farming breaks the cycle, so the soil system breaks down.

Desertification in the Sahel

The Sahel region lies to the south of the Sahara Desert. Its climate is more moist than the desert climate, but its rainfall is low, and it has a long dry season.

This climate supports a natural vegetation system called 'savanna' – grassland, with some trees and shrubs. The grass grows rapidly in the hot wet season, then the leaves of the grass die in the dry season. This forms a dense mat, protecting the roots from drought. They survive, to grow again when it next rains. Trees that survive here either store water in their trunks, or develop very long root systems to seek for water over a wide area.

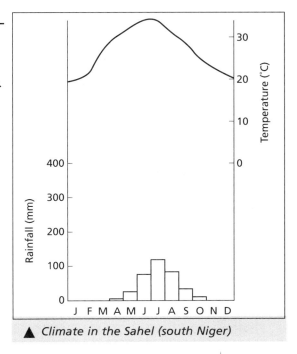

▲ *Climate in the Sahel (south Niger)*

The vegetation is not the same over the whole savanna. It forms a transition zone between the desert to the north and the rainforest to the south. The grassland is very sparse on the semi-desert margins, growing more lush, and with more trees, nearer the rainforest.

Nomadic farming

The drier parts of the Sahel have been home to nomadic pastoral farmers for hundreds of years. They follow a seasonal pattern of movement, seeking supplies of pasture and water for their cattle. The cattle provide the people with most of their needs – food, skins, and transport. They also provide men with status, as cattle are a sign of wealth and power. Any other needs are met by trading with settled farmers who live in wetter areas to the south.

This way of life forces people to live carefully in their environment. In good years, with plenty of rainfall, the grass grows well and supports the cattle. Calves survive and the herds grow. But in bad years there is not enough grass, so the weaker cattle and calves die. A balance is kept between the land, the herd size, and the human population. The human

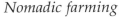

DID YOU KNOW ?

In the dry season the dry savanna grassland is often burnt, either by natural fires or by herdsmen who burn the dead grass to encourage new shoots to grow. Trees that survive here have to resist fire, as well as drought.

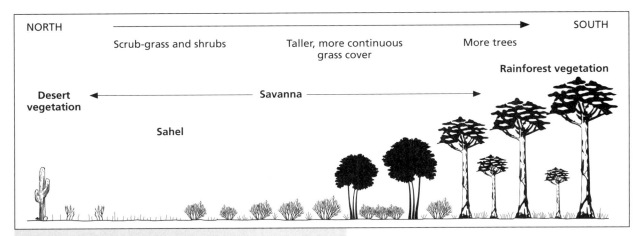

▲ *Cross-section through a savanna vegetation region*

population cannot grow too large, because they cannot be supported if the land cannot support increased numbers of cattle.

During the last 50 years many changes have upset this balance:

- new medicines and treatments have cut the death rate, so population has grown

- emergency feeding has cut the death rate in the dry years, and increased population totals

- veterinary treatment has kept more cattle alive

- herdsmen have been encouraged to trade their cattle, to provide food for the growing urban markets, so they have to keep more cattle

- some pasture land has been taken over to grow cash crops, which upsets the old balance between people and land

- nomads are stopped from travelling to some areas, because national borders are patrolled more strictly now; this also upsets nomadic systems.

As the population of people and cattle increased, the area of grassland available was reduced. This put pressure on the vegetation, and on the soil that supported it.

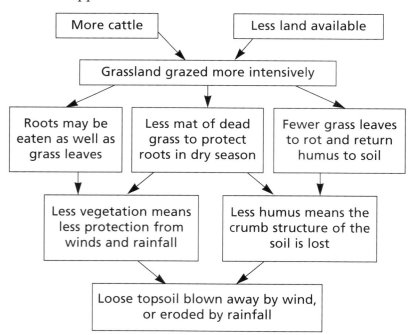

This process started in small areas with very dry conditions, which were seriously over-stocked with cattle. However, once it started it spread quickly. As soon as one area became unfit for grazing, the cattle became more concentrated on the smaller area of suitable land. This area too was soon over-grazed.

Some people were forced to abandon their way of life completely, and move to the cities. Other groups of herders moved south, to the wetter crop-growing areas, threatening these parts too.

Focus Point 2

Cover the page. List three ways that the herdsmen used their cattle.

Focus Point 3

Cover the page. List some of the reasons why the cattle herds often overgraze the land now.

This traditional way of life was a 'sustainable' use of the environment. Not all modern developments are sustainable.

Hints and Tips!

If you ever need to draw a flow diagram like this in an exam, do not waste time drawing boxes with a ruler. But remember, the arrows are very important. They show how processes link together, and they *must* be put in properly.

Unfortunately, land that has been over-grazed does not recover. There are several possible reasons for this:

- As the roots have been destroyed, the grass does not regrow.

- If the soil has been badly eroded, vegetation cannot grow back.

- The loss of vegetation means rainfall is not taken up by roots and re-evaporated. Instead it runs off to rivers more quickly, and flows out of the region. This has probably led to reduced rainfall in areas that already had low rainfall.

Desertification means the spread of desert into areas that used to be useful. The process of vegetation loss, soil erosion and reduction of rainfall leads to desertification.

The European Union's Common Agriculture Policy

The European Union (EU) was first set up in 1956. (It was called the European Economic Community then.) Europe was still recovering from the damage and losses of the Second World War. The war had caused food shortages in many parts of Europe. This was partly because the continent had come to rely on importing cheap food from abroad. The EU was determined to make Europe self-sufficient in food, so the Common Agricultural Policy (CAP) was set up.

One of the CAP's main aims was to increase the efficiency of farming. It was hoped that more food could be produced from the best land, using a smaller work-force. In some of the best farming areas, like East Anglia, the CAP encouraged farmers to:

- use more fertilizers, pesticides, etc.

- increase mechanization on farms

- concentrate on arable crops in areas that had previously had pastoral or mixed farms

- join small farms together to make bigger units

- increase field sizes, by pulling up hedges, to allow machines to be used more efficiently.

These policies all helped to increase production. The CAP was very successful in making Europe self-sufficient. Indeed it was so successful that the famous 'mountains' of excess food built up. Unfortunately, as well as increasing production, the policies listed above all helped to cause soil erosion.

Focus Point 4

Why does desertification lead to urbanization?

Hints and Tips!

If you are asked to name an area of desertification in your exam, remember:

Desertification takes place on the edge of deserts. Loss of vegetation and soil erosion in tropical rainforests is *not* desertification.

There have been a lot of complaints about the CAP. It was very successful at first. However, it caused problems because once self-sufficiency had been achieved it should have been changed. This did not happen, the CAP got out of control, and the food mountains grew.

Increased use of fertilizer, reduced use of manure $\longrightarrow$	Less humus returned to the soil, so crumb structure was damaged
Increased mechanization $\longrightarrow$	Heavy machinery compressed soil; less infiltration of rainwater; more run-off
Reduction of pastoral farming, grass ploughed up for crops $\longrightarrow$	Ploughing leaves soil without vegetation cover, so no roots to protect soil
Removal of hedges $\longrightarrow$	Nothing to break the force of the wind, so erosion is increased

Hints and Tips!

The arrows on the table show links or connections. High-level answers in a geography exam need to explain links and connections as clearly as possible.

Soil erosion in East Anglia

The erosion in East Anglia never became as serious as in some parts of the world, like the Sahel or the 'Dust Bowl' of the USA, but increased output from the land was damaging the soil. In the 1990s the CAP has attempted to stop or even reverse the damage that was done to the soil. Now the CAP encourages farmers to reduce the intensity of their farming by:

- paying subsidies to farmers who replant hedgerows

- paying them to 'set aside' land – they are paid money for leaving a percentage of their land unused, which allows the soil to recover, and provides land for wildlife

- encouraging 'diversification' or finding new uses for land, such as nature reserves and land for leisure, rather than using enormous areas for single crops.

Exam practice

(a) Describe one way the CAP tried to increase production on farms. (5 lines)

(b) Explain how this caused soil erosion. (5 lines)

(c) Describe what has been done to reduce that problem. (5 lines)

(10 marks)

 **ocus Point 5**

Read all three parts of this question before you start to answer it. The different parts of your answer must be linked together.

Farming and the physical environment

Key idea 3
The influence of the physical environment on farming differs according to the level of economic development.

Scale
Regional
International

Expanded key idea
In less economically developed countries (LEDCs) farmers do not have much money to invest in the land. They are very dependent on the natural environment, because they can do little to alter conditions.

In more economically developed countries (MEDCs) farmers can often afford to invest large amounts of money in the land, to overcome the constraints of the natural environment. However, even in MEDCs there are areas that are so difficult that it is not worth investing much money in the land; and some farmers in LEDCs are now investing a lot of money in the land.

Case Study

Intensive and extensive land use in the Netherlands

Most of the western part of the Netherlands lies below sea level. It has been reclaimed since the seventeenth century. At first Dutch traders invested their profits in new land, by building dykes and pumping out the water. In the twentieth century the state has taken over the main responsibility for reclaiming land and protecting it from floods.

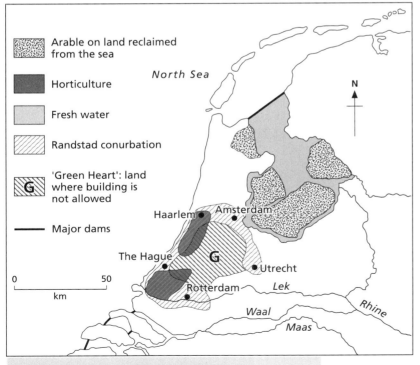

▲ *Land use in the western Netherlands*

Note
Traditionally the Dutch used windmills to pump water off the land. Now they usually use diesel or electric pumps. But in some places the winds blowing off the sea are now being used to drive wind turbines. The traditional energy source is providing 'clean' electricity.

One Dutch market gardener is quoted as saying, 'I want nothing to do with soil. It is dirty and difficult to control. It is better to grow my crops on blotting paper soaked with water which contains exactly the right chemicals for my crops.'

Once so much money has been spent overcoming the physical environment it is essential that the land is used intensively, so that the investment pays off. This means that agriculture is carefully designed to meet the needs of the large, rich market in nearby Randstad, and to export crops to the other urban markets of the EU. Market gardeners in this area invest so much money in their farms that the natural conditions of soil and climate can be almost totally ignored.

A horticulture system

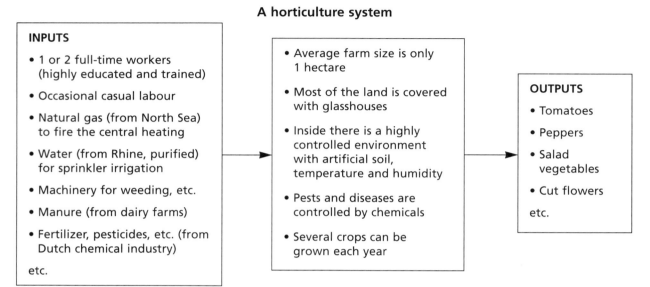

INPUTS

- 1 or 2 full-time workers (highly educated and trained)
- Occasional casual labour
- Natural gas (from North Sea) to fire the central heating
- Water (from Rhine, purified) for sprinkler irrigation
- Machinery for weeding, etc.
- Manure (from dairy farms)
- Fertilizer, pesticides, etc. (from Dutch chemical industry)

etc.

- Average farm size is only 1 hectare
- Most of the land is covered with glasshouses
- Inside there is a highly controlled environment with artificial soil, temperature and humidity
- Pests and diseases are controlled by chemicals
- Several crops can be grown each year

OUTPUTS

- Tomatoes
- Peppers
- Salad vegetables
- Cut flowers

etc.

A contrasting region in the Netherlands

In the east of the Netherlands there is an area where agriculture has never developed so intensively. This is the heathland or 'Geest', low hills about 100m above sea level. They were formed from material left by the melting ice at the end of the Ice Age. The soils are infertile, and because they are sandy, they are permeable and cannot hold moisture for plant growth.

Some areas of the heath have been improved by adding lots of manure, but the soils have never been made fertile enough to be very profitable. Most of the area has never been farmed intensively. Instead it is left for:

- forestry
- rough grazing for sheep
- nature reserves
- open heathland for leisure – walking, cycling, etc.
- military training.

ocus Point 1

How do market gardeners in the Netherlands get over the natural limits of the environment? Refer to:
(a) temperature
(b) moisture
(c) soil nutrients.

Note These uses could all be described as 'extensive' land uses: large areas/ low inputs/low outputs.

Contrasts in LEDCs

Market gardeners in the Netherlands can grow salad crops in winter, even though the area's climate is far too cold for them to be grown outside. This is possible because people in the Netherlands have capital (money) to invest. This is not usually possible in LEDCs, because people here do not have capital available and are much more dependent on the natural conditions of the soil and climate.

Examples

One example illustrating the close relationship between poor people and environmental conditions was given on pages 57–59, where the farming system of nomadic pastoralists in West Africa was described. The nomads have always been forced to migrate in their search for pasture and water for their cattle. Once their traditional migration pattern was disrupted, their farming system often deteriorated as the land was not able to support them, and desertification was the result.

In contrast, the text on pages 113–115 describes how farmers in Kenya are adapting their traditional farming system to make use of the environment to grow vegetables for the European market. This produces profits that can be re-invested in the land.

The section on rice farming in the Punjab on pages 53–55 describes an area in an LEDC where farmers have been able to alter the environment, to some extent. They can grow rice where the climate is really too dry, because they have been able to organize and pay for irrigation water, new seeds, fertilizers, etc. as part of the Green Revolution.

However, most farmers in the sub-continent cannot alter their environment like this. Farmers in Bangladesh, who live on the floodplains of the Ganges, depend on the seasonal river floods (see page 49). If the monsoon rains are late, the growing season is cut short, and food supply is reduced. If rains are heavier than normal and the floods are higher, they can bring disaster. So can cyclones. People here cannot control the sea and the rivers as the Dutch people can. Their lives are far more directly ruled by the environment.

Hints and Tips!

All the examples in this section show how good planning of revision means that you can use one case study to illustrate several key ideas. This makes learning more efficient.

ocus Point 2

Describe one example of farming in an LEDC where the system is almost totally dominated by the environment.

Describe another example where people in an LEDC have invested money to give them some control over the natural environment.

B ii) Natural hazards and human responses

Earthquakes and volcanoes

Key idea 4 Crustal instability may cause problems for people as it is responsible for the occurrence of earthquakes and volcanoes.	**Scale** *Regional* *International* *Global*

Expanded key idea

The crust of the Earth is divided into a number of separate sections, known as plates. These float on the mantle and convection currents in the mantle move them across the surface. When two plates touch, at a plate margin, they can move in different directions. This leads to instability, causing earthquakes and volcanoes. Over a long period these processes cause mountain building. They are great hazards to people, but good management can reduce the hazard.

The Earth's plates and plate margins

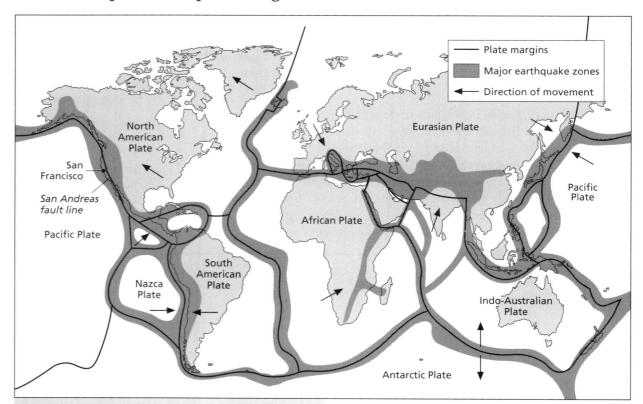

▲ *The Earth's largest plates and earthquake zones*

Plate margins are classified according to the way the plates move in relation to each other. Their names are based on whether new plate material is being formed or old plate is being destroyed.

Direction of movement	Name	Process
Plates move apart	Constructive margin	New plate is constructed
Plates move together	Destructive margin	Old plate is destroyed
Plates move side by side	Conservative, or slip margin	No plate constructed, and none destroyed

Different activities take place at each type of margin, and these cause different types and levels of hazard to people.

Name	What happens	Result
Constructive margin (diagram (a))	As the plates move apart they leave a gap. Pressure is reduced on the magma below.	Magma rushes up to fill the gap, causing volcanoes. These are usually basic lava types, and are not very explosive.
Destructive margin (diagram (b))	Plates move together and the denser plate sinks beneath the less dense one.	Plates rub against each other causing friction which melts the one that sinks. The melted rock, under pressure, flows back to the surface forming volcanoes. The friction between the plates builds up, until sudden slips cause earthquakes.
Slip margins (diagram (c))	Plates move side by side, in different directions, or at different speeds.	These plates rub against each other, causing earthquakes. There is no gap, and no pressure on the mantle, so volcanoes do not happen.

Hints and Tips!

Remember, 'destructive margins' did not get their name because they destroy life and property. They were so named because plate material is destroyed. If you keep that in mind it is easier to remember the names of all three types of margin.

ocus Point 1

Name the three types of margin. Say whether earthquakes and/or volcanoes are common at each one.

Give an example of each, using the map on page 64.

(a) Constructive margin

▲ *Constructive and destructive plate margins*

Hints and Tips!

Practising how to draw diagrams like this is very useful revision. You learn lots of information, but it is also a useful skill to be able to draw good, quick diagrams in the exam.

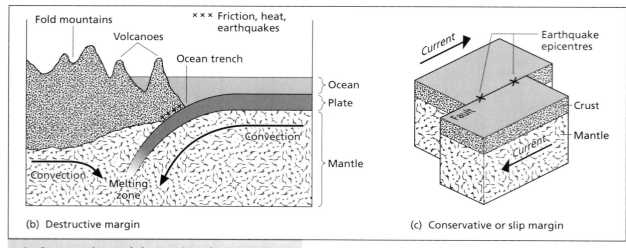

(b) Destructive margin   (c) Conservative or slip margin

▲ *Constructive and destructive plate margins*

Case Study

Earthquakes in California and Japan

California and Japan are two of the most economically developed areas in the world, but people in both countries have to live with the constant threat of earthquakes. California lies on the conservative margin where the Pacific Plate slides alongside the North American Plate. Japan is close to the destructive margin, where the Pacific Plate plunges beneath the Eurasian Plate.

California
San Francisco was almost totally destroyed by an earthquake in 1906. Many of its buildings were made of wood, and some were destroyed by the movement of the 'quake, but even more were burnt down by the fire that followed. This was uncontrollable, because gas and electricity mains had been destroyed and coal fires in houses burned out of control. The fire brigade could do little, because roads had been blocked. Even when they could get to fires the water mains were often burst, so there was no water to put out the fires.

Still, the city was rebuilt in the same place. People knew that further 'quakes could happen there, but the site was ideal for building a port. As the city has grown, many precautions have been taken to prevent the earthquake hazard causing further disasters:

- Buildings designed with very strong foundations. They will sway during an earth movement, whereas normal, rigid buildings would collapse.

- Some skyscrapers have a pyramid shape, with a broad base and narrow top. This increases stability.

- Roads and bridges designed to resist earthquakes – so many vehicles use the freeway systems that a 'quake during rush-hour would be disastrous if all the roads collapsed.

One woman leapt out of her bath when the 1906 earthquake struck. She ran into the street naked, and was promptly arrested. It is good to know that the police had their priorities right in an emergency!

ocus Point 2

Cover the page. List five precautions taken in San Francisco to reduce the loss of life and property in an earthquake.

- Gas mains have automatic cut-out systems. If pressure falls because of a broken pipe, the gas automatically stops flowing.

- All inhabitants taught earthquake drills. Schools have earthquake practices, just as British schools have fire practices.

- Well-trained and equipped emergency services. They have earth-moving equipment and fire engines that are designed to get through blocked streets.

When San Francisco suffered another major earthquake in 1989, during the rush-hour, the precautions worked so well that relatively few people died (67 people) and 2000 were made homeless. With the shock measuring 6.9 on the Richter scale, there would have been much more serious damage if the city had not been so well prepared.

Japan

Japan's worst disaster was in 1923, when Tokyo was hit by an earthquake. It is thought that up to 100 000 people were killed in that one event. Now the people of Japan have learned to plan for and live with the hazard. They have a reputation for being well prepared for earthquakes. They have 'Disaster Day' on 1 September every year, when everyone practises their emergency procedures. Tokyo has been well planned to withstand the hazard. One apartment complex for about 10 000 people has been built to be earthquake-proof, but it is also designed as a firebreak. It should stop fires spreading through the surrounding, older, wooden houses. Large areas next to the buildings have been left clear, to provide evacuation space which will be safe from fire and collapsing buildings.

Unfortunately, Japan's most recent severe earthquake (7.2 on the Richter scale) centred on the city of Kobe, in January 1995. Many buildings and freeways were destroyed, despite the building regulations, and 5000 people were killed. Fires spread after the first shocks, and although the emergency services were trained and equipped, they could not reach them. They burned for up to three days, and 250 000 people were left homeless. Because it was winter this caused great suffering.

One unexpected result of this 'quake was the damage done to Japan's economy. Many firms in the Kobe region make parts for larger firms throughout Japan. The country's efficient transport system means that these parts can be delivered very quickly, 'just in time' to be used in production. Big firms do not therefore need to hold large stocks of parts. Unfortunately the earthquake disrupted many of Kobe's firms, and the whole region's transport system. Without parts from Kobe, many of the big firms had to stop, or slow down their factories for several weeks, even months.

Many people think that rush-hour is the most dangerous time for an earthquake to strike San Francisco. The city has so many flyovers, road and rail bridges and underground rail lines that it is feared thousands of people could be trapped and crushed in cars or trains in an earthquake.

ocus Point 3

List four examples of the human and economic damage caused by the Kobe earthquake.

Earthquake prediction

If people could predict exactly when and where earthquakes were going to happen, many lives could be saved. Seismologists spend a lot of time trying to make predictions. So far they have had very little success in giving warnings that are accurate enough to evacuate populations and save them from the disasters. Now, though, some seismologists are trying a new approach.

Every earthquake starts at a **focus**. Waves travel outwards from the focus, and cause the shaking of the Earth that brings the damage. The waves travel at between 6 and 13km per second. If a focus is about 50km away from a city, and if the very first tremor can be identified, this means that between 4 and 8 seconds' warning can be given. If messages can be sent automatically, over computer links to vital control centres, then:

- gas supplies can be cut off immediately

- nuclear reactors can be made safe (or at least safer)

- the bullet train in Japan (for example) can be stopped, or slowed down, reducing the risk of derailment.

If the focus is a bit further away, and the warning time is 20 seconds:

- some people can get out of buildings

- fire engines can be moved out of their stations, so they do not get trapped

- emergency procedures can be started in hospital operation theatres

and so on.

These short warnings may not sound much but, with careful organization, they could be enough to make some very important moves and save many lives.

In 1976 Chinese scientists did predict an earthquake. They evacuated tens of thousands of people and probably saved thousands of lives. Unfortunately they have not been able to predict other 'quakes since then – but maybe scientists will be able to predict accurately in the near future.

Questions

Volcanic eruptions

Refer to a volcanic area that you have studied.

1 Describe the nature of the eruptions.

2 Explain what causes the eruptions.

3 Describe the consequences, both bad and good.

Weather and climate

Key ideas 5–6   Scale
Extreme weather and climate conditions pose problems for people. Responses   *Local*
to these hazards vary with different degrees of economic development.   *Regional*
                                                                              International

Expanded key idea
Tropical storms are examples of extreme weather events, which occur in certain predictable
and clearly defined areas. These include some highly developed regions, where people are
usually well prepared to manage the storms and their consequences. Storms also happen in
less developed areas that are less well prepared to cope.

The areas of origin of tropical storms

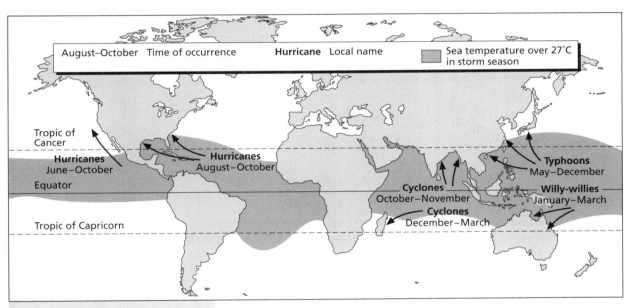

▲ *Hurricanes around the world*

It can be seen from the map that the areas where tropical storms start
are found:

- over the oceans
- between 5° and 20° north and south of the Equator
- usually close to the east coast of continents.

It should also be noted that they start when:

- ocean temperatures are at least 27°C
- the water is heated to a depth of several metres
- it is late summer or early autumn, when sea temperatures are at
  their highest.

Someone once said:
'Tropical storms are
like old men with bad
feet. They like to sit
with their feet in
warm water.'

The map also shows that the storms, once they have formed:

- move westwards, towards the land
- follow erratic and unpredictable courses
- swing polewards when they reach land
- usually die out soon after they have reached land.

The causes of tropical storms

The hot sea contains an enormous reservoir of energy, and it is this that powers storms.

1 Air resting on the surface of water becomes very hot. It also becomes very humid, because it contains a lot of water vapour, evaporated from the warm surface.

2 The hot humid air rises, and cools. This causes condensation and cloud formation.

3 The rising air creates a low pressure area, so new air is drawn in to fill this area. As this new air passes over the warm sea surface it too becomes hot and moist.

4 A strong system of winds develops, with air rushing in to the centre of the storm.

5 The rotation of the Earth means that the winds do not blow straight. They follow curving paths, with the winds circulating in towards the centre.

6 The whole circulating system then starts to move westwards, towards the land.

7 When the system crosses the coast it loses its source of heat and moisture. This means that it soon loses its energy. It dies out, usually leaving a deep low pressure area with strong winds – but these are not as disastrous as the winds in the storm.

The structure of a tropical storm

Diagram (a) on the next page shows a map of the surface winds blowing in towards the centre, or 'eye', of a storm. Photo (b) is a satellite view of a similar storm. It shows the banks of cloud round the eye of the storm. Diagram (c) is a cross-section through the same storm. The table below the cross-section shows how the weather changes as a storm passes.

Focus Point 1

Tropical storms always start over the sea.

Give three facts to describe the state of the sea where they start.

Give three facts to describe the way that storms move.

Hints and Tips!

It is sometimes easier to learn a complex set of information by breaking it up into smaller parts. In this case:

Stages 1–3 = birth of a storm

Stages 4–5 = development of the storm

Stages 6–7 = old age and death of the storm

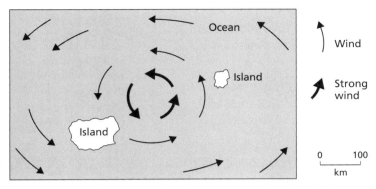

(a) Map of a tropical storm or hurricane in the northern hemisphere

(b) Satellite view of a similar storm

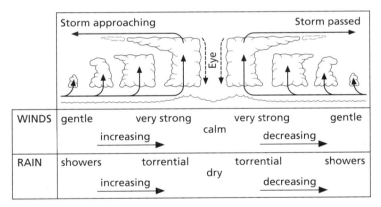

(c) Weather and waves during the passage of a tropical storm

◀ *Features of a tropical storm, or hurricane*

Focus Point 2

Describe how the weather changes as a storm passes. Mention:

- the approach and early stages
- the climax of the storm
- the eye
- the retreat of the storm
- wind
- cloud
- rain
- sea conditions.

Managing the effects of tropical storms

These storms contain enormous amounts of energy. Some estimates suggest that, in a single day, a storm can release as much energy as would be released by the explosion of 500 000 atom bombs! It is obviously impossible for people to control such powerful forces. However, careful management can reduce the damaging effects by:

- long-term planning in areas where storms are common
- studying and tracking storms once they form
- action as the storm approaches, to minimize damage.

Planning for cyclones in Bangladesh

In Bangladesh, cyclones can be especially damaging. They blow from the Bay of Bengal, and certain aspects of the local geography make their effects particularly serious.

- The Bay is funnel-shaped (see map on page 47). As the winds move northwards they are funnelled by the coastline, and this increases their strength. The surging waves blown by the wind are also concentrated, and become higher and stronger.

- The coast and delta land is very low-lying. This means that it offers little protection from the wind or waves.

- The fertile delta land is ideal for rice growing, so it is very densely populated.

- Bangladesh is a very poor country, with little money to spend on warning systems, coastal defences, or evacuation arrangements.

The Flood Action Plan (FAP) is an attempt by the Bangladeshi authorities and international aid donors to tackle the area's problems. Projects that are being researched, and which may be built over the next 30 years, include:

- improved satellite weather forecasting, to allow better prediction

- building and reinforcing coastal banks to protect land and people from floods

- raising the mounds that people live on, so that they are above the level of the highest floods

- improving roads so that aid can be delivered to affected areas more easily

- building concrete storm shelters, like the one shown below.

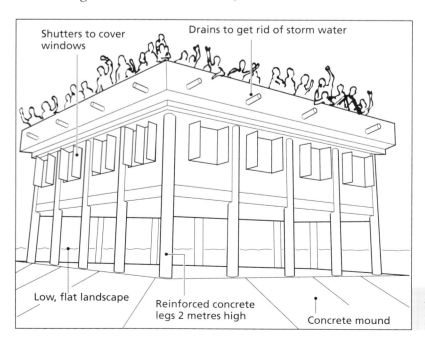

Shutters to cover windows

Drains to get rid of storm water

Low, flat landscape

Reinforced concrete legs 2 metres high

Concrete mound

◀ *A tropical cyclone shelter in Bangladesh*

Hints and Tips!

To help you structure your revision, and to plan your exam answers, it is often useful to consider physical factors and human/economic factors separately. This section illustrates this technique well. Divide the causes into two physical and two human.

Focus Point 3

List four aspects of the human and physical geography of Bangladesh that make tropical storms here particularly dangerous.

List four ways of reducing the damage done by cyclones in Bangladesh's Flood Action Plan.

Questions

Tropical storms

In developed countries, better provision can often be made to plan for storms. Revise a case study of a storm which affected an MEDC.

Refer to:
- long-term planning
- tracking the storm as it approaches
- action as a storm gets near.

See page 102 for another example of the effects of a tropical storm.

B iii) Leisure and the environment

Key ideas 7–9 **Scale**

Increased leisure time and prosperity has resulted in increased use of areas of *Local*
great scenic attraction. Some areas are in danger of being overused, so *Regional*
careful planning and management is needed to resolve conflicting demands *International*
on the countryside.

Expanded key idea

Since the Second World War, people in MEDCs have had more leisure time, and more money
to spend on leisure pursuits. New developments in transport have made people more able to
travel for leisure pursuits. This has led to large numbers of people going to certain areas that
have a hot, dry climate and/or an attractive environment. There has been overuse of some
areas, damaging the very environment that attracted people to the area in the first place.

Increased leisure time and mobility

Since the Second World War, people in Britain have had more leisure
time because:

- most workers now have longer periods of paid holiday

- most workers have a shorter working week than they used to

- housework is less time-consuming because of labour-saving equipment.

People are able to travel more easily because:

- far more families have cars now

- the road system has improved, especially with the building of
  motorways

- networks of inter-city coaches now cover most of the country
  (although many local bus services have declined)

- air fares have become much cheaper

- large planes, especially jumbo jets, can move people abroad in far
  greater numbers.

In addition, the average person has far more 'disposable wealth' (or
spare money after essential costs have been paid). This means more
money to spend on leisure.

The National Parks

There are eleven National Parks in England and Wales, shown on the
map on page 42. Most are in upland areas in the north and west,
although the last one designated as a National Park was The Broads, a
flat, low-lying area in East Anglia.

Note This
refers to the
average. Some
people still work
very long hours.

**ocus
Point 1**

Try naming all
eleven National
Parks. Then look
back at the map on
page 42 and check
your answers.
Finally, turn back to
this page and try
again.

The first National Parks in Britain were set up soon after the Second World War. They had two main aims:

• To conserve areas of beautiful and remote countryside.

• To encourage people to use these areas for leisure.

It should be clear that, right from the start, there was a potential conflict between these two aims, because:

one of the best ways to conserve the land, is to stop large numbers of people from using it.

if large numbers of people are encouraged to use the land they will almost certainly bring changes.

Another problem arose right from the start. The National Park authorities do not own the land in the Parks. They just have responsibility for helping to plan how the land is used. In fact most of the land is owned by farmers. Large areas are also owned by forestry companies, water boards, the National Trust, the army, quarrying companies, private householders, and so on. It was clear that there could very easily be conflict between the needs of the landowners and the needs of people wanting to use the land for leisure. So the park authorities developed a new aim:

• To try to plan the use of the land so that the needs of all the potential users are met, and so that conflict between the different users is reduced as much as possible.

The development and management of 'honeypots'

Some of the most difficult problems for the planners of the Parks have arisen at what are described as 'honeypot' sites. This name arose from the phrase 'they flock there like bees round a honeypot'. Examples are given below.

Type of site	Honeypot site	National Park
Ancient monument	Housesteads on the Roman Wall	Northumberland
Spectacular scenery	Malham Cove Snowdon summit	Yorkshire Dales Snowdonia
Publishing/TV link	Grosmont ('Heartbeat' country) Beatrix Potter's farm	North Yorkshire Moors Lake District
Small town	Eyam, Bakewell Okehampton	Peak District Dartmoor

It should be noted that all the examples in the table above (except one) have good road links. This is almost essential if a site is to develop into a honeypot. Even the summit of Snowdon has easy access. Although many visitors walk or climb to the top, there is a mountain railway which carries many less hardy, less energetic visitors straight to the summit.

◆ This could be described as 'the National Park paradox'. It seems impossible to achieve both aims at the same time.

◆ Remember, jobs in tourism are usually only seasonal. They cannot be relied on to offer a wage all year round.

Hints and Tips!

This table is an attempt to classify honeypot sites. Putting them in groups like this is a way of making learning easier, and of helping to give a structure to exam answers.

ocus Points 2 and 3

◆ You may well have visited or studied other honeypot sites. Where do they fit on this table?

◆ Does the Snowdon railway fit in with both, one or neither of the original aims of the National Parks?

When a site becomes a honeypot many problems can result, but the tourists can also bring benefits to the local area.

Problems	Benefits
• Litter	• Trade for local shops
• Lack of parking spaces, and spread of parked cars onto verges, farmland, etc.	• Money provided for investment in improved facilities, e.g. roads
• Road congestion in the neighbourhood	• Jobs for local people
• Lack of toilets	• Farmers can sell produce such as eggs to visitors
• Overuse of footpaths leading to erosion of land surface	• Spare farm buildings can be converted into holiday cottages
• Conflict with farmers if tourists damaging hedges, gates, etc.	• B & B guests can be taken in

ocus Point 4

Choose one of the honeypots listed on page 75, or one of your own examples. Make two lists: people who benefit from the existence of the honeypot, and those who suffer.

Questions

Honeypot sites in the UK

1 Give an example of a honeypot location.

2 Describe its attractions.

3 Describe the problems caused by its overuse, explaining how this causes conflict with other land users.

4 Discuss some possible management solutions.

Leisure and the environment of the Mediterranean coast

Many of the changes that have led to increased pressure on National Parks have also caused management problems for coastal resorts around the Mediterranean. The growth of free time, increased affluence, and the development of package holidays have led to a boom in the leisure industry all round the coast of southern Europe and in parts of north Africa.

The two graphs on the next page show the temperature and rainfall for Falmouth in south-west Cornwall and Cartagena in south-east Spain.

Both these places have beautiful scenery, sandy beaches and many other attractions for holidaymakers, but Spanish resorts can rely on the hot, dry Mediterranean climate in summer. Spain also has the attraction of lower prices because of the low average wages paid to workers in the tourist industry.

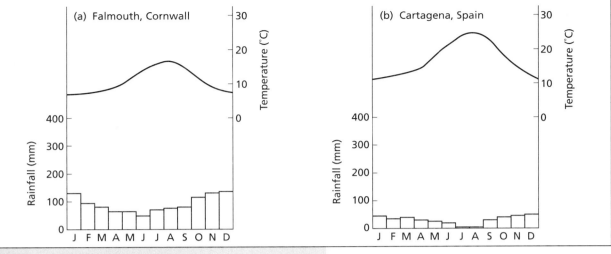

▲ *Climate graphs for (a) Falmouth and (b) Cartagena*

Advantages of development

The physical and economic attractions of the resorts around the Mediterranean coast have led to very rapid growth of the tourist industry. The boom has brought rapid development and improvements in wages for many people. The infrastructure of roads, water supply, airports, trade networks, etc. has also been improved, bringing many benefits to local people.

Problems of development

Development has also caused problems. In many places it has damaged the environment. Scenery has been altered, and often spoilt; water has been polluted; traditional industries such as fishing have been damaged; traditional cultures have been threatened; and so on. All this has been done to develop tourism, but fashions can easily change, and old resorts may be abandoned if the market for holidays moves somewhere else.

ocus Point 6

Use the graphs to complete the table.

	Falmouth (Cornwall)	Cartagena (Spain)
Average July temperature (°C)		
Average August temperature (°C)		
Average July rainfall total (mm)		
Average August rainfall total (mm)		

What does your table suggest about the number of hours of sunshine and cloud in the two resorts?

What does it suggest about sea temperatures in the two resorts?

uestions

The tourist industry abroad

1 Name a region that you have studied which has an 'international' tourist industry, e.g. the Mediterranean coast.

2 List its attractions for tourists.

3 Describe some of the benefits and problems caused by the growth of the tourist industry in that area.

The tourist industry has always depended on fashion. In England resorts like Bognor Regis and Lyme Regis took advantage of visits by the King. They gained publicity by adding 'Regis' (Latin for 'King') to their original names.

Exam practice

Choose any resort or holiday area that you have studied. It could be in the UK or another country.

(a) Describe the natural attractions of the area. Refer to both climate and scenery. (6 lines 6 marks)

(b) List three ways that money has been invested to provide tourist facilities in the area. (3 lines 3 marks)

(c) Explain how the tourist industry has brought both benefits and problems to your chosen area. (15 lines 8 marks)

For further details about the benefits and problems brought by the tourist industry, refer to page 116.

B iv) Industry and the environment

Key ideas 10–12

Industrial activity brings social and economic gains for individuals and nations. It can also have an impact on the environment, which can be beneficial or damaging. The physical environment can hinder economic development.

Scale
Local
Regional
International
Global

Expanded key idea

Development of resources always brings change. Some groups and individuals benefit from those changes, but other groups and individuals may suffer losses. It is important to understand the values and attitudes of the people who are affected by the changes. Then it may be possible to plan development to increase the advantages and reduce the disadvantages.

Development is also interrelated with the environment. The environment offers certain possibilities for economic development, but it may also present difficulties which must be overcome. If development goes ahead, the environment will be changed. Sensible management tries to reduce damage to the environment.

Case study

Resources and the environment – Alaskan oil

The development of Alaska's oil illustrates the key ideas in this section perfectly. The oil that was discovered here is a very valuable resource. Its development offered enormous benefits to many people, but also presented a threat to a very special, unspoilt environment. The actual development process has been carried out very carefully, and the developers have gone to great expense to try to conserve the wilderness area. Despite this care and expense, accidents have happened, and damage has been done. Maybe this was inevitable.

The resource
Oil was discovered in Prudhoe Bay, Alaska in 1968. The oilfield lies below the North Slope of Alaska, partly below the land surface, and partly below the sea bed.

Development work, and the building of the pipeline, meant that it was not available for use until 1997. Supplies from the oilfield were expected to last for 30 years, but further discoveries have extended its life. Now, about 33 per cent of the USA's oil comes from Alaska. Alaska also produces 12 per cent of the country's natural gas.

Problems of the environment around Prudhoe Bay

Prudhoe Bay lies inside the Arctic Circle. This causes a number of problems for the oil companies:

At present, the USA uses about 33 per cent of all the oil produced in the world.

Note Imagine what would happen if a building was built over permafrost. The weight of the structure would put pressure on the permafrost, and melt it. The foundations would turn to mud, and the whole thing could collapse.

- In winter the area has 24 hours of darkness. This made drilling and other work on the site very difficult.

- Temperatures are very low. Average January temperatures are about –15°C and even in July they do not reach 10°C.

- The low temperatures mean that the soil is **permafrost**. It is permanently frozen to a depth of several metres. The surface layer thaws in summer, but the meltwater cannot drain away because the permafrost lower down makes the soil impermeable. The trapped meltwater makes the surface very boggy and unstable.

- Low temperatures also mean the sea is frozen for most of the year.

- Even when the sea is not completely frozen, there are many icebergs.

The pipeline and its environment

The frozen sea made it impossible to ship the oil out by tanker. The only way that it could be exported was by pipeline, but there were enormous environmental problems with this solution. If a pipeline was to be built it had to meet the demands of the well-organized environmental protection groups in the area. The ecosystem, called **tundra**, is very fragile. If it is damaged it may take 50 or more years to

Problems	Solutions
• The extreme cold might freeze the oil, and stop it flowing.	Heat the oil to 80°C before it enters it enters the pipeline.
• The heat from the oil could melt the permafrost.	Insulate the pipe in special concrete casing.
• Digging a trench in the permafrost may damage the tundra.	In areas with very delicate tundra, build the pipeline on stilts above the ground.
• A pipeline on stilts may block the caribou migration routes.	Build the stilts 3m high where it is necessary.
• The pipeline has to cross several mountain ranges.	Put pumping stations along the route to push the oil over the mountains.
• The mountains in the south are in an active earthquake zone.	Put flexible sections in the pipeline, so that it can move from side to side and up and down without breaking.
• The pipeline still might break.	Have automatic cut-out systems, which stop the oil flowing if pressure in the pipe falls too low.
• Construction work could destroy tundra. Bulldozer tracks could still be visible 30 years later.	Have strict rules for construction teams, with big penalties if they break them, and big bonuses if they comply.

Focus Point 1

Cover the page. Explain what is meant by 'permafrost'. Then describe four other problems of exploiting oil in this area.

Hints and Tips!

When you try to learn this table, underline one key word or phrase in each problem. Learn these. Then each word should trigger the whole sentence, and the solution that goes with it.

Focus Point 2

Cover the page. List four problems faced by the pipeline builders. For each problem describe how they tried to solve it.

recover, because plants grow so slowly in the harsh climate. The problems were so serious that it seemed as though a pipeline would be uneconomic.

Then, in the early 1970s, the price of oil rose very rapidly because of the actions of the Organization of Petroleum Exporting Countries (OPEC). This suddenly made the Alaska oil much more valuable, and the USA faced a massive crisis if new oil supplies could not be brought to the country. This made the cost of the pipeline more acceptable. It could now be built to meet the needs of environmental conservation and still make a profit and meet industrial and domestic oil needs in the USA. The problems could be solved, or at least it was hoped they could. So the pipeline was built, at a cost of US$7.7 billion. It ran from Prudhoe Bay to Valdez, on the warmer, southern coast of Alaska. Supertankers could easily come in here, collect the oil, and ship it south to California.

The price followed the law of supply and demand. OPEC cut the supply of oil, but the USA still demanded the same amount. This pushed the price up.

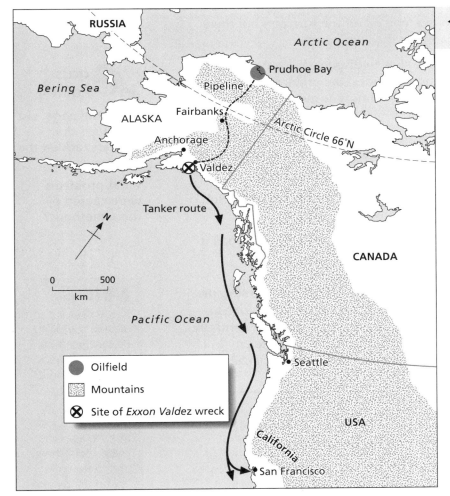

◀ *Oil from Alaska: pipeline and tanker route*

California is USA's most populous state. Los Angeles has the highest rate of car ownership of all the world's major cities.

Hints and Tips!

Oil in Alaska is a compulsory case study for this syllabus. Make sure that you learn it – thoroughly.

The south coast of Alaska is still a very important, unspoilt wild environment. It is home to such wildlife as sea otters, seals, sea lions, killer whales and many species of sea birds. Any tankers operating in this area have to follow very strict rules to prevent spillages. They have to stay in certain 'safe' areas. The tanker companies promised that all tankers would have 'double hulls' with two thicknesses of steel plates, so if one layer was damaged in an accident the oil would not spill.

The *Exxon Valdez* disaster

In March 1989 the *Exxon Valdez* ran aground on rocks off the Alaska coast. The tanker was 50km off course. Some people say it was avoiding icebergs, others say it was taking a short cut to save time and increase profits. It is rumoured that the captain was in his cabin, drunk, at the time of the accident.

A total of 12 million gallons of oil were spilt, creating a slick which was carried towards the coast, threatening its whole ecosystem. It also endangered fish stocks – one of the few sources of wealth in Alaska other than oil. Despite the risk, the oil companies and authorities were not well prepared for the spill. Several methods were tried to get rid of the oil:

- 'Skimmer boats' were used to scoop oil off the surface – but there were only four boats available for the whole area.

- Chemicals were sprayed on the slick to disperse it – but environmentalists say that this just 'hides' the problem. The oil sinks to the sea bed, and the chemicals do almost as much damage to wildlife as the oil does.

- Floating booms were put round the slick to stop it spreading, but there were not enough booms, and they were used too late, when the oil had already spread.

- Attempts were made to burn the oil, but this created air pollution, and could not deal with all the oil anyway.

- Finally, workers waited for the oil to come ashore, then scooped it off the beaches, and sprayed it with detergents.

In fact, experts now say that, once the company had failed to stop the oil spreading in the first place, there was little that could be done to help. It was probably best to leave the oil to be broken down naturally. Although this is a slow process, especially in such cold water, it probably does less damage to the ecosystem than any use of chemicals.

Focus Point 3

Describe two precautions that the tanker companies promised to follow to prevent oil spills.

Why did the environment make such precautions necessary?

Focus Point 4

Cover the page. List four ways that workers tackled the spill.

What problems were caused by these methods?

Note This method of leaving the oil to be dispersed by natural methods seemed to work quite well after the *Braer* oil spill off the Shetlands; but the sea was not as cold there, and there were strong winds and currents to help break up the oil.

Questions

Development of industry

1 Name a local or small-scale example where the development of industry has brought both benefits and problems to the area.

2 Explain why the industry developed in that particular place.

3 Who benefited? Explain how they benefited.

4 Who suffered? Explain how and why their problems were created.

5 What attempts were made to reduce the problems?

6 Will the industry, and the benefits and problems, last for a long time, or are they only temporary and short-term?

Exam practice

Suggest how the following people or groups might view the development of oil in Alaska now, 20 years after it first started to be delivered:

- a car salesman in San Francisco

- a fisherman living in southern Alaska

- a real estate saleswoman (estate agent) in Valdez

- a tribe of Native Americans, traditional hunters, some of whom got temporary labouring jobs when the pipeline was being built

- the Professor of Ecology and Conservation at the University of Alaska

- the Professor of Petroleum Economics at the same university.

Environmental problems for the future

Key idea 13   Scale

The benefits of economic activity can result in environmental problems   *Local*
for future generations. There is an increasing awareness of the responsibilities   *Regional*
of stewardship, the need for conservation, and the importance of   *Global*
sustainable development.

Expanded key idea

All economic activity has some effect on the environment. As it happens it may seem
unimportant, but the effects can build up, and work in unexpected ways. For example,
burning fossil fuels releases gases into the atmosphere. Now, it is realized that this has
caused a build-up of carbon dioxide in the atmosphere, which is probably causing global
warming. This has many consequences for the world's weather. Not all of these are fully
understood, but the changes may cause serious problems. The release of other gases from
burning coal probably causes acid rain.

Is global warming happening?

This is a subject that is surrounded with controversy. Since the 1960s
some scientists have said that global warming is happening, and some
have said that it is not. Those who think it is have not all agreed about
the speed of change. Some have said it is due to human factors; others
believe it is mainly natural.

There have also been disagreements about whether anything can be
done to stop or reduce the warming.

The graph shows the changes in global temperatures. It is quite clear
now that there have been two periods of very rapid warming, from
1910 to 1940 and again from 1975 to the present.

Note Global
warming is not an
essential topic on
the syllabus.
It is used here as
*one possible
example* of an
environmental
problem.

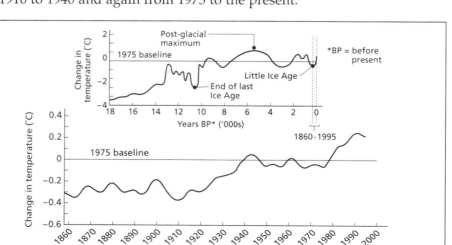

▲ *Change in average global temperature compared with 1975 figure*

Hints and Tips!

Warning! Be very
careful what you
say about global
warming. Do not
state anything too
strongly. You
cannot prove or
disprove any of
the theories, but
you can present
evidence, and
*suggest what
might be
happening.*

What would be the impact of global warming?

Obviously temperatures would increase, but not evenly all over the globe. The icecaps would melt faster, although some people think that higher temperatures would cause greater evaporation, leading to increased snowfall, so the ice sheets might not actually shrink in size.

Even if the icecaps do not melt, sea level could rise by 1–2 metres over the next 50 years. This could be caused by expansion of the water, due to its increased temperature. This would lead to flooding of many coastal areas. Some island states might disappear altogether. Even more worrying is the threat to many of the world's great food-growing areas on low-lying river floodplains, such as the Ganges delta in Bangladesh. Many great port cities are also found on coasts.

The movement of the wind and pressure belts would lead to a change in the distribution of rainfall over the continents. This could lead to massive changes in agricultural production.

There would certainly be an increase in violent, unstable weather conditions. It is thought that the frequency and strength of tropical storms is already increasing. Floods and droughts may be happening more often too.

If global warming *is* happening, what is its cause?

The 'greenhouse effect' is a natural process. Some gases, particularly carbon dioxide, but also methane, water vapour and nitrous oxide, allow the sun's rays to pass through the atmosphere and warm the Earth. Then they trap some of the heat and stop it being re-radiated. Without this process the Earth would be too cold for life as we know it.

However, since the Industrial Revolution, people have been burning fossil fuels in ever increasing quantities, and this releases carbon dioxide into the atmosphere. This is probably adding to the natural greenhouse effect.

The graph below shows how much the various regions of the world are contributing to the carbon dioxide in the atmosphere, and how their rates of emission are changing.

Note Some people suggest that global warming might make temperatures in the UK *fall*. This could happen if melting of the Arctic icecap causes changes to the pattern of ocean currents, which could divert the warm North Atlantic Drift away from the British Isles.

Focus Point 1

Re-read this section and pick out five changes that could happen as a result of global warming.

Hints and Tips!

Make sure you understand that the greenhouse effect is a natural process that has been *increased* by human actions.

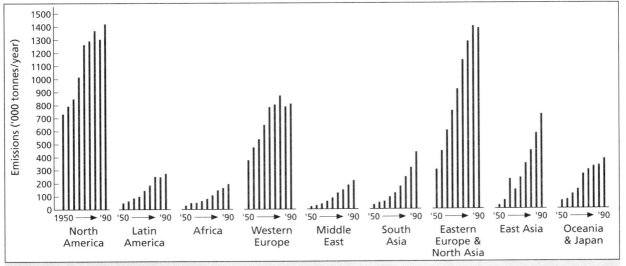

▲ *Changing carbon emissions from major world regions*

What the graph shows
The figures show several points quite clearly.

- More economically developed countries (MEDCs) in North America and Europe have always produced more carbon emissions than the less economically developed countries (LEDCs).

- Emissions by the MEDCs increased rapidly at first (in the 1950s and 1960s) but slowed down after about 1970.

- In western Europe it seems emissions are falling now.

- Emissions by LEDCs are low but rising.

- They are rising particularly fast in east and south Asia.

- East and south Asia are also very densely populated. Their emissions per person are still far lower than emissions per person in the MEDCs.

What can be done to reduce the threat of global warming?

Most world leaders now accept that global warming is a threat, and that something needs to be done about it. It seems certain that responsibility for action will lie mainly with the MEDCs. They have been, and still are, the main polluters. In addition, they can better afford to bring in the changes needed. There are two different types of response to the threat.

1   Try to prevent, or slow down, warming by controlling emissions of greenhouse gases.

2   Plan now to reduce the damaging effects of warming.

How can warming be prevented or slowed down?
- At the Earth Summit in 1992, it was agreed that by 2010 countries should reduce their emissions to 1990 levels. Many, but not all, countries have agreed to this.

- The Kyoto Conference in 1997 was an attempt to go further than this, and to start cutting emissions. Europe argued for a 15 per cent cut to 1990 levels by 2010. The USA argued against this, saying that it will lead to far too many job losses.

- The main way to reduce emissions is to reduce the burning of coal and oil. To help this people can:
  - use more renewable energy
  - use more natural gas, which emits less carbon than coal does
  - conserve energy in the home and in industry
  - plan transport policies to reduce the use of cars and lorries
  - invest in new technology to improve efficiency in producing and using energy
  - share new technology, with developments in MEDCs being made available cheaply for use in LEDCs.

Focus Point 2

For each area on the graph:

(a) How much carbon is being emitted now?

(b) How much did its emissions grow between 1950 and 1990?

(c) In the last ten years, have its emissions grown faster, slower, stayed about the same, or shrunk?

Hints and Tips!

Remember these two headings, and use them to structure your revision and to plan exam answers.

Note Countries attending the Kyoto Conference did agree to cut emissions by the year 2010. Some countries, mainly in the EU, said they would cut them sooner and by more than the treaty suggested. The Conference also agreed that big polluters would be allowed to buy pollution 'allowances', but a lot of pressure was put on the USA to make it try to cut its pollution.

Energy use must be planned so that it is sustainable. This does not just mean that people in MEDCs should be able to sustain their high standards of living. It means that people in LEDCs should be encouraged to raise their standards of living, but they should be helped to do this in the most energy-efficient way possible.

How can we plan to reduce the effects of warming?
Even the most optimistic forecasts for the reduction of emissions accept that some warming will still happen. Therefore the problem must be managed. This means that over the next 50 years or so, people will have to do the following:

- Plan for flood control. The Thames Barrage is one example of how this is being done already. However, the problem in places like Bangladesh is on a far larger scale.

- Plan for water supply in areas of possible drought. Already the UK has suffered water shortages in several areas. Even quite wet countries like ours need to introduce very efficient national water grids, so that the resources can be used efficiently.

- Attempt to 'drought-proof' agriculture. Development of strains of plants that use less water is probably important. More important is to develop techniques of farming that use water less wastefully. Conservation of water, like conservation of energy, will become more and more important.

The management of land and water resources, as for energy resources, should be based on planning for sustainable development or 'stewardship', for people in all parts of the world.

Focus Point 3

Cover the page. List four ways that people can reduce the emissions of greenhouse gases.

Focus Point 4

Cover the page. List three ways that people could be planning to cope with the effects of global warming.

Questions

Development and the environment

1 Name a small-scale or local area example where development is causing environmental problems.

2 Explain how the environment is threatened by this development.

3 Explain how the development can be managed to reduce the threat to the environment. Refer to sustainable development in your answer.

3 The impact of economic change

A What is economic change?

> ### Key idea 1
> Employment can be classified as primary, secondary or tertiary, and the proportion of the workforce in each sector changes as countries become more developed. Countries can be classified in terms of economic development.
>
> **Scale**
> *Local*
> *Regional*
> *International*
> *Global*
>
> ### Expanded key idea
> • Primary employment is work producing raw materials. Secondary employment processes raw materials and manufactures finished products. Tertiary employment does not produce things, but provides a service.
>
> • Less economically developed countries (LEDCs) usually have a large proportion of the workforce in primary employment, but more economically developed countries (MEDCs) usually have a high proportion of people working in the tertiary sector.
>
> • Economic development causes many other changes in countries' populations. For instance, development can lead to changes in the age structure of the population, and in its geographic distribution.

The employment classification

Employment can be divided into three (or sometimes four) groups or categories.

1 **Primary employment** produces raw materials from the land. It includes:

  - farming   - fishing   - forestry   - mining.

2 **Secondary employment** takes the raw materials and manufactures them to produce finished products. Most of this work takes place in factories. It includes:

  - processing iron ore to make steel

  - using steel to make components, such as car engines

  - assembling the components to make cars

  - spray-painting cars to finish them for sale.

3 **Tertiary employment** provides a service. It does not involve a finished product, but it often means dealing with people. It includes an enormous range of jobs, for example:

- accountant
- designer
- greengrocer
- bus driver
- electrician
- hairdresser
- chiropodist
- football professional
- zoo keeper

Employment and economic development

In most LEDCs a large proportion of the population work in the primary sector. Most of the people in countries like Kenya are near-subsistence farmers, only producing small amounts of produce for sale in the market. In some other LEDCs a large proportion of the labour force work in mines or on commercial farms, producing raw materials for export to MEDCs. Copper miners in Zambia (see page 115) and cotton growers in Egypt are examples of such raw material producers.

As a country develops its economy, people move from the primary sector into secondary employment. Jobs are created in industry, because this produces more wealth. There is more profit in exporting expensive manufactured goods than in exporting raw materials for someone else to process.

The 'tiger economies' like Taiwan and the Philippines are going through the process of industrialization now. They are 'newly industrializing countries' or NICs. South Korea has gone through this phase and is a 'newly industrialized country'.

In countries with more mature industrial economies, the number of people working in factories starts to fall. Increased mechanization means fewer workers are needed. In these countries, like the UK and France, more and more people work in services.

	Employment (%)		
	Primary	**Secondary**	**Tertiary**
France	4	27	69
Kenya	54	8	38
South Korea	13	33	54

Population structure and economic development

In many countries it has been observed that, as the economy develops, the population structure goes through a series of changes. These changes are called the **demographic transition**.

Stage 1
In countries with a very simple subsistence economy, healthcare is usually poor. This means that the death rate is high, especially amongst the most vulnerable group, babies and children under five.

To compensate for this, couples usually have many babies, hoping that one or two will survive, so the birth rate is also high.

Note Some people say there should be a fourth group – **quaternary employment**. This would include all the people working in information technology. At present they are included in the tertiary group.

 **ocus Point 1**

Cover the page. Write out brief definitions of primary, secondary and tertiary activities. (Note that when writing a definition you should not need to use examples.)

Note This point about the 'tiger economies' was written in early 1998 and was true then. By May 1998 the Philippines, and other Asian countries, were in serious economic difficulties. Check the situation when you study this. It will have changed.

Hints and Tips!

Death rate is the number of deaths in a year, per thousand population (written as ‰).

A high birth rate and a high death rate means that the population stays low. It may fall suddenly in bad years of drought, famine or disease. Then it may rise slowly again as conditions improve, only to fall again when the next difficult time arrives.

Stage 2

As the economy develops, money becomes available for better health-care – nurses, medicines, better sanitation, drier and warmer housing, better childcare, etc. The death rate starts to fall, slowly at first, but then faster as conditions improve. Usually the birth rate stays high, because people are used to having many children. It takes time for the 'culture of the high birth rate' to change.

The high birth rate and falling death rate combine to cause population increase. It starts growing slowly, but the rate of growth speeds up. This can cause a 'population explosion'.

Stage 3

People keep on having large numbers of children as long as they feel there is a need for them. Reasons for a high birth rate include:

- Children can support parents in their old age.

- Children can work on farms, in industry or in many services. Their income can make the difference between survival and disaster for many families.

So the birth rate starts to fall when people no longer feel that they *need* to have large families. In other words, it falls as the standard of living of the poor people starts to rise.

In this stage the death rate is low, and although the birth rate is falling it is still higher than the death rate. The population total still grows, but the rate of growth slows down.

Stage 4

In most MEDCs the birth rate and the death rate are both low. Health-care is good and reliable. People expect their children to survive, so they know they can keep families small. In fact, in wealthy countries children have become very expensive, because people expect to pay for them to have a high standard of housing, food, leisure, travel, education and other things. People have a strong *motive* to limit their families, and family planning gives them the *means* to do this.

In MEDCs, with low birth rates and low death rates, the total population is usually steady. Total population is often high but these countries have strong economies, which can support the large numbers, as long as they do not increase any more.

Hints and Tips!

Birth rate is expressed in terms of the number of live births in a year, per thousand population (‰).

◆ In the 1960s the world's population was increasing very rapidly. This was not because people had started to 'breed like rabbits' but because they were no longer 'dying like flies'.

◆ Contraceptives and family planning advice alone will not reduce the birth rate. It only falls when couples realize *they* can benefit by not having a large family.

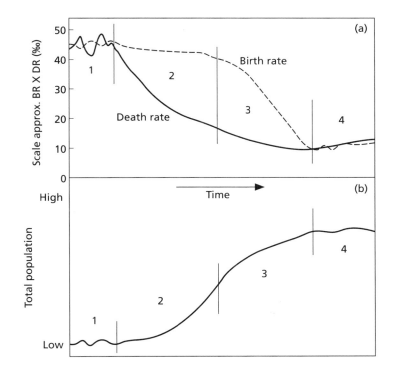

The demographic transition
(a) Birth and death rates
(b) Total population

Hints and Tips!
At Stage 3 the *population increase* slows down – but population is still rising. Students often get confused about this and say that population starts to fall. **Be careful!** Do not make this mistake.

Exam practice

(a) Complete this table to show the changes during the demographic transition. (You may use words from the list at the bottom of the page, but Higher tier candidates should not need to use them.)

Stage	1	2	3	4
Death rate				
Birth rate				
Total population				

high high high high, but now stable low low low rising at an increasing rate			
starts to fall starts to fall still falling still rising, but at slower rate			

(8 marks)

(b) Explain what causes the change from Stage 2 to Stage 3 of the demographic transition. (3 lines 2 marks)

(c) Explain what causes the change from Stage 3 to Stage 4. (3 lines 2 marks)

Case study

Brazil, the demographic transition and migration

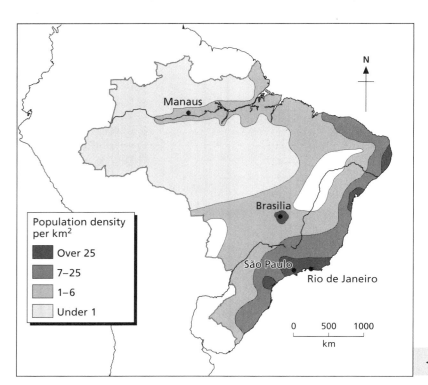

◀ *Brazil: population density*

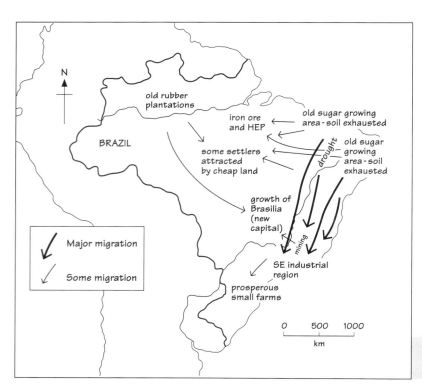

◀ *Brazil: pushes and pulls of migration*

Brazil has the largest population in South America and is the eighth largest of all the countries in the world. The following figures show its growth from 1980 to 1994, and its predicted growth up to 2004.

Brazil	Total population (millions)	Total increase in 10-year period (in millions)	% increase in 10-year period
1980	121	31 (1980–1990)	26
1990	152	30 (1990–2000)	20
1994	164	26 (1994–2004)	16
2000	182		
2004	190		

The rate of increase was high, but it is falling, and predictions show that the rate of increase will continue to fall. Brazil is in Stage 3 of the demographic transition. However, the situation is not the same in all parts of the country. Brazil has a very uneven distribution of population and of economic development – see the maps on page 92.

Changes in population density

- Population has grown very fast in some areas.

- Some poor areas do not have enough resources to cope with population growth. This causes population pressure.

- Economic development has offered big opportunities in some areas. This has led to great pressure to migrate in Brazil, and people have moved *from* areas of population pressure *to* areas of economic opportunity.

B Changes in the location of economic activity

> **Key idea 1**   **Scale**
> The location of manufacturing may be influenced by many economic factors,   *Local*
> but political considerations and the social and leisure environment are   *Regional*
> becoming increasingly important.   *International*
>
> **Expanded key idea**
> The study of industrial location used to concentrate on five main factors:
>
> 1 raw materials   2 energy   3 labour   4 market
> 5 transport costs (to get 1–3 to the factory and 4 take the product to market).
>
> These are still important, but transport has become much more efficient in the last 50 years,
> so its costs have become less important. At the same time political influences and
> considerations for the environment have become more important.

Case study

The iron and steel industry in the UK and the EU

Iron and steel was the most important industry in Britain during the
Industrial Revolution. It provided basic materials needed by all other
industries. Its location has changed many times since then, as different
factors have become more or less important.

Early iron industry
Before 1600 the industry was found in the Weald and the Forest of
Dean. It used small, local deposits of iron ore and charcoal as its power
source. They were bulky and could not be moved far with the poor
transport systems of the time.

Later iron industry
In the period to 1700, iron production spread to Sheffield. There were
ore deposits nearby, and fast-flowing streams from the Pennines could
be used for power.

Early steel industry
In 1709 Derby discovered that coke could be used to smelt iron ore. The
industry used enormous quantities of raw materials:

8 tonnes of coal + 4 tonnes of ore = 1 tonne of steel

so the industry developed on the coalfields, where 'black band' ore was
found in between the coal seams. South Wales, Sheffield, central
Scotland and north-east England became important in this period.
When the ore ran out in these areas the industry survived because:

- so much money had been invested in the steelworks

- there was a skilled labour force

DID YOU KNOW?

◆ Iron ore is a rock
that contains the
element iron,
combined with other
elements. These have
to be removed by
melting the rock.
During this process,
called 'smelting', the
other impurities
combine with lime to
form 'slag' or waste.

◆ Steel is iron that has
combined with a small
amount of carbon
(and sometimes with
other elements).
Different steels can be
made which are
stronger than iron, or
more easily shaped, or
do not rust so easily,
etc.

• it was cheaper to move imported iron ore to the coalfields.

When an industry stays in a place even when the original reason for its location has gone, it is known as **industrial inertia**.

Later steel industry

In 1879 the 'Gilchrist–Thomas process' was developed. This allowed ore with a high phosphorus content to be smelted. Such ore was found in the Jurassic limestone hills, so new steelworks were opened in Scunthorpe and Corby. The ore was impure, and contained much waste, so it was cheaper to move coal to the ore.

The modern steel industry

By 1950 several very important changes had taken place.

• Most of the UK's iron ore was exhausted. Most ore had to be imported. It was brought in by bulk carriers, which needed deepwater ports to dock.

• Improvements in technology meant that much less coal was needed to make every tonne of steel.

• New technology meant that steel could be produced most cheaply in massive, integrated steelworks.

• Competition increased in the world market. Steel from the Far East and eastern Europe, where labour costs were lower, had taken many of the traditional markets for British steel.

Focus Point 1

Write one sentence to summarize the reason why the early steel industry developed at coalfield locations.

Explain why 'industrial inertia' meant it stayed here, even when its main raw material had run out.

Terminals for the bulk carriers have highly automated unloading systems. They cut costs by ensuring that the ships can turn round quickly and go back for another load.

▼ *Location of iron and steel in Great Britain, 1967 and 1997*

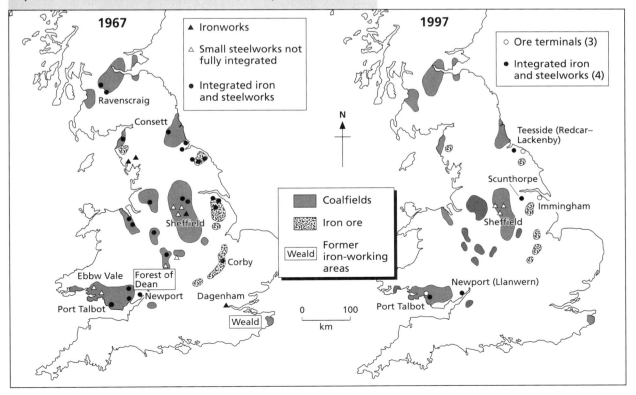

- The government (both in the UK and the EU) has played a much bigger role in deciding where plants should be located. Sometimes they have done this by telling the industry where to locate. At other times they have influenced the industry, by paying grants and subsidies. Government policy has also influenced which steelworks should be closed.

There are now only four large integrated steelworks left in the UK. They are all on the coast, except Scunthorpe which has very close rail links to a major ore terminal. Investment has been concentrated in these four plants so that steel can be produced cheaply enough to compete on the world market. This has meant that some traditional steelmaking areas have lost all their industry. This has caused great social problems in some areas, such as Ravenscraig in Scotland. Unfortunately the government could not continue to subsidize these plants. In the long run it was better for them to lose their steelworks and try to use

Hints and Tips!

Try to learn how the steel industry developed over the past centuries. If you are short of time, it is most important to learn where it is located now, and why.

ocus Point 2

Name the UK's four integrated steelworks. Explain why they are located in those places.

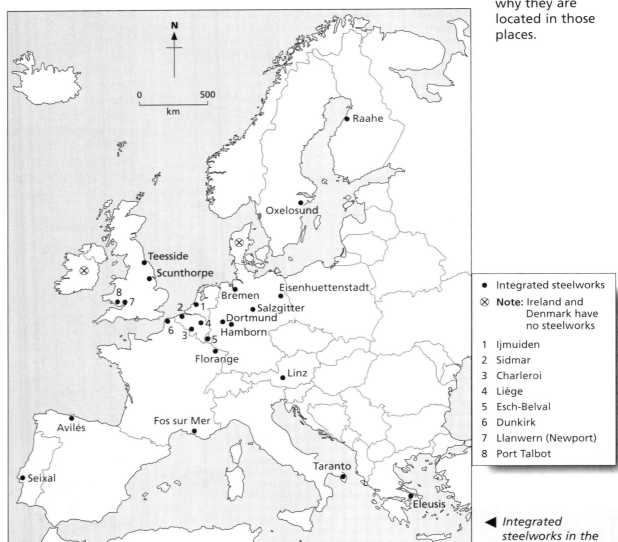

◄ *Integrated steelworks in the European Union*

government and EU grants to attract modern, profitable industries and services.

The map on page 96 shows how similar considerations have affected changes in the European steel industry since economic integration of Europe has led to planning of the industry across the whole of the EU.

The map on page 96 shows

Hints and Tips!

Be aware of the general pattern of Europe's steel industry for your exam – but you only need to learn about one area in detail.

Questions

The automobile industry in the UK

Describe the factors that influence the location of the industry. You should refer in detail to at least one plant, and briefly compare several different plants. For example, you should compare:
- a traditional manufacturing area, such as Oxford or Coventry
- a plant built in the 1960s in an area of high unemployment, e.g. Halewood
- a recent plant, built with Japanese 'inward investment' money.

High-technology industry in the UK

A computer is an expensive item, costing hundreds or even thousands of pounds. Yet the raw materials it contains are probably only worth a few pounds. So why is it so expensive? What are we paying for? Well, the money pays for:

- the highly educated designers and programmers who developed the computer and its component parts, such as microchips and processors – in other words, research and development costs

- the cost of developing the software

- the skilled labour that made the components, and then assembled them

- the cost of plant and machinery in the factories

- advertising and promotion

- transport of the very fragile finished product

- sales staff, and the after-sales technical back-up staff

and so on.

This all goes to show that the old rules of industrial location do not apply to modern, high-tech industry. Computer manufacture does not have to be located where the raw materials or the coal to supply power can be brought together. Instead, industries like this are located in two types of area. The work is often split between 'development' sites and 'assembly' sites.

Development sites need:

- access to highly educated, creative thinkers – these are usually found in and around universities

- an attractive environment, where these workers will be willing to work

- contact with other people in high-tech industry, who can share ideas and stimulate further development work

- easy access to the rest of the world (via airports) so that ideas can be shared, and potential buyers and providers of components and programs can easily keep in contact

- good road access, by fast, uncongested routes.

Assembly sites need:

- skilled and semi-skilled workers

- reasonably low wage rates

- government subsidies which are often paid to firms that locate in areas with high unemployment

- easy contact with the development sites, and with the market – this means that good road access is essential.

The M4 Corridor and the Western Crescent

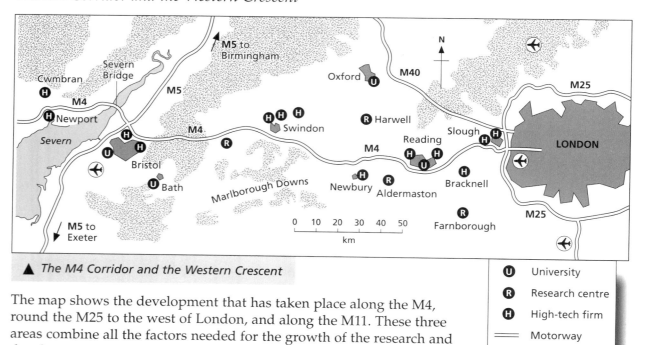

▲ *The M4 Corridor and the Western Crescent*

Ⓤ	University
Ⓡ	Research centre
Ⓗ	High-tech firm
═══	Motorway
✈	Airport
🔶	Town
░░	Hills

The map shows the development that has taken place along the M4, round the M25 to the west of London, and along the M11. These three areas combine all the factors needed for the growth of the research and development sector of high-tech industry. Once established in this area the high-tech industry has multiplied.

Note The Cambridge Science Park, linked to the university, is probably the UK's best example.

ocus Point 3

Go through this list relating to development sites, linking each point to a specific fact about the M4 Corridor. In other words – link the theory to a real-life example.

The map also shows how high-tech industry has spread into South Wales. This area has many of the attractions needed for development work, although it is not as well placed as Berkshire at the other end of the M4. However, South Wales has high unemployment and a good pool of skilled and semi-skilled workers, and grants are available for new firms setting up here. This makes the area attractive for the assembly plants that make the finished products which have been designed in the development plants elsewhere.

ocus Point 4

Several assembly plants developed in South Wales. Why were there plenty of workers available here? Which declining industries had they come from?

People say that 'Silicon Valley' in California grew because so many people left big IT firms to set up their own businesses to develop their new ideas. Similar developments have happened in the M4 Corridor.

The tertiary sector

Key idea 2

Scale

The location of tertiary activities is influenced by such factors as accessibility and the size of markets.

Local
Regional

Expanded key idea

Shops and other kinds of services have to be located in places where they can make a profit, so they have to attract enough customers, and sell enough goods. Choice of the best location depends on the type of shop. Different types of shops seek different types of location.

How do shops make profits?

Near the school where I used to work there are two 'shops'. One sells sweets and newspapers; the other is a Jaguar car showroom. The owners have different strategies for making a profit.

Sweet shop	Car showroom
Sells a lot of goods, making a small profit on each sale.	Sells a small number of items making a large profit on each sale.
Hopes that the people will shop there regularly – every day even.	Knows that even best customers will only buy once a year.
Most of customers live in the local area, or attend the school.	There are not many Jaguar buyers in the local area, so has to attract people from a very wide area.
People wanting to buy sweets never travel long distances just to buy sweets.	People wanting a new Jag do not mind making a special journey to a specialist showroom.

Note The sweet shop is a 'convenience shop'. There are many of these and they are found close to people's homes. The Jaguar showroom is a 'specialist shop'. There are far fewer of these, and people often make long journeys to get to them.

The shoe shop is a 'comparison shop'. These are often grouped together in town centres.

There also used to be a shoe shop near the school. It closed down several years ago. People would not come to this little shop in the suburbs when they could easily travel into the town centre, where there were lots of shoe shops with a big variety of styles at a wide range of prices, but offering good value for money.

The concepts of 'threshold' and 'range'

Every shop, shopping centre or service has its own **threshold population**. This is the number of people who are needed in the market area of the shop to make it profitable.

The Jaguar showroom has a very large threshold population, because the people in any area do not buy many Jaguars. The newsagent and sweet shop only has a small market area, because people buy sweets and newspapers regularly, so the shop can make a profit with a fairly small threshold population.

Every shop also has its own **range**. This is the distance that people are prepared to travel to visit the shop. As the example shows, Jaguar buyers have a long range. They do not visit the showroom very often, so they are prepared to make a long journey for its specialist products. The sweet shop has a much smaller range. Even chocaholics will not travel miles and miles for their purchases!

Both the successful shops have a threshold population which lives within range of the shop. Both are profitable. Even Mrs Choudhury who runs the sweet shop can afford to drive a Jaguar!

The shoe shop had to close down because people would not bother travelling a mile to get to this little shop when they could get much better choice and value by travelling three miles into town. Its threshold was bigger than its range. It was not profitable. It could not survive.

Examples of threshold and range

Type of shop	Threshold popn (approx.)	Range (approx.)	
• Corner shop	1000	0.5km	easy walking distance
• Group of 4 or 5 small shops in a suburb	5000	1km	walk or short drive
• small supermarket, e.g. Spar	7500	2km	walk or short drive
• large supermarket, e.g. Tesco	25 000	10km	car usually needed to carry a week's shopping
• town centre shops	100 000	20km	serve town and its surrounding region
• regional centre, e.g. Meadowhall	500 000	50km	serves several towns and their surrounding regions
• city centre shops, e.g. Birmingham	1 000 000	100km	serve a whole conurbation and other towns as well
• London's West End shops	10 000 000	500km	serve the whole country

Focus Points 1, 2 and 3

◆ For each shop in this table, say whether it is convenience, comparison or specialist:

- off-licence
- fancy dress hire
- take-away restaurant
- ladies' fashion clothes
- video hire
- records and video sales
- surf boards and skis
- electrical goods
- newsagents.

◆ Write precise definitions of:

- the threshold population of a shop
- the range of the goods sold in a shop.

◆ Try to add your own local examples to each level of this table (except London, which applies to the whole of the country).

The larger shops and centres in this table are called **high order** centres. Note that:

- the threshold and range both increase for high order centres
- high order centres are less common than low order centres
- high order centres are more widely spaced than low order centres
- the high order centres rely on cars or public transport to survive. As car ownership becomes more common, many people do not bother to visit local, low order centres. These are being driven out of business by the big supermarkets and the regional shopping centres (see page 30).

C Economic growth and decline

> **Key idea 1**
> There are many reasons why a region or country might experience economic problems.
>
> **Scale**
> *Local*
> *Regional*
>
> **Expanded key idea**
> Some areas, regions or countries go through periods of economic decline. There are many different causes of such decline. They include bad weather, exhaustion of resources, lack of money for investment, rapid population growth, fall in demand and political influences.

Bad weather damages employment opportunities

To people living in a more economically developed country (MEDC) it may seem odd to say that bad weather can have a major effect on a country's economy. However, in many less economically developed countries (LEDCs), bad weather can be devastating.

Guadeloupe
Guadeloupe is a small island country in the West Indies. It has a population of about 345 000 people, about the same as a large town in the UK. Many of the people live in small towns or large villages, but they still rely on agriculture. Many grow subsistence crops, but they also have two main cash crops, bananas and sugar cane, mainly for export to the European Union. Much of the sugar is processed to make rum, which is the country's main manufactured export.

Although it is in the West Indies, Guadeloupe is actually an overseas *département* of France. It elects a member of the French parliament and has very close links with the EU.

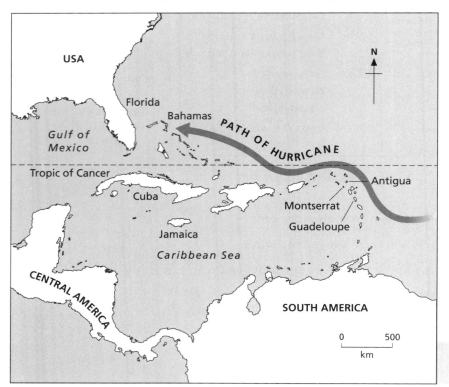

◀ *The track of Hurricane Hugo*

In 1989 the island lay right in the path of Hurricane Hugo, the region's worst hurricane for ten years. The storm brought winds which gusted to over 200km/hr, and these destroyed large areas of farmland. Subsistence crops were badly damaged and huge areas of sugar cane were flattened, but it was the banana trees that suffered the worst damage. Trees in the storm's path were simply snapped off leaving stumps about one metre high.

Fewer than 20 people were killed, but thousands were made homeless, and the whole basis of the island's economy was damaged. Short-term aid was needed to ensure that the people survived, but it has been estimated that it will take ten years, and millions of dollars' worth of foreign aid, for the country's economy to recover from the effects of that 24-hour period of bad weather. (See page 70 for details of the causes of tropical storms.)

(See page 70 for details of the causes of tropical storms.)

Exhaustion of resources damages employment opportunities

The Northumberland and Durham coalfield has been one of the main centres of heavy industry in Britain since the Industrial Revolution. Coal and iron ore were both mined here, and were used to make iron and steel. Then coal was used to power factories that turned the steel into ships, railway engines, tanks, power station turbines, girders for bridges, and a wide variety of smaller products. Local coal was also used in industries such as aluminium refining, pottery, chemical manufacture, and so on.

The coalmining industry reached a peak in the period between 1910 and 1925, but was still a vital part of the region's economy in 1947. Since then its decline has seemed unstoppable.

	1947	1994
Number of collieries	188	0
Number of workers	148 000	2000 (mainly in opencast mines)

In 1996 one mine, at Ellington in Northumberland, was re-opened but now, in 1998, its future is under threat again.

Many of the pits in this area were in villages and small towns where the mining industry provided many of the jobs and brought most of the money into the area. When the pits closed there was little alternative work. Some people left the area, and others stayed but with little or no opportunity for paid work. The settlements went into spirals of decline.

Reasons for closures
Clearly, the effect of pit closures on these communities was devastating. Social problems followed the economic decline. Yet to describe the problem as 'exhaustion of resources' is an oversimplification. There is still a lot of coal left under the ground in the area's coalfield. The reasons for the closures include:

- The most accessible coal has been mined.

Note **Warning!**
Experts fear that global warming could make extreme weather events, like hurricanes, far more common in future.

These industries can all be described as 'heavy industry'. Because of their bulk the transport costs were high. They tended to locate close to the coalfields to cut transport costs.

Hints and Tips!

Question Is it necessary to learn these statistics?

Answer You will not get a question in the exam that asks 'How many coalmines were there in Durham in 1947?' But you might be asked to 'Explain why your chosen region has suffered economic decline.' Then, knowledge like this will help you to write a high-level answer.

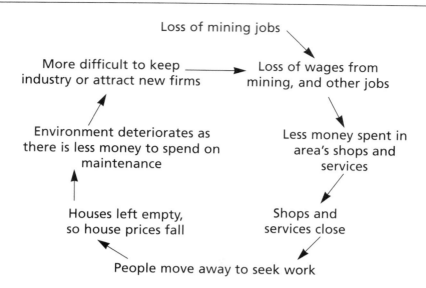

ocus Point 1

Cover up the page. List at least five of the stages in the 'spiral of decline' that often follows closure of an area's biggest employer.

- The coal that remains is deeper, so it is more expensive to mine.
- It is more dangerous to mine the coal that remains.
- Less demand for coal in the steel industry (see page 95).
- The change to using gas in electric power stations.
- There has also been a small increase in the use of nuclear power and renewable energy.
- There has been pressure to reduce the use of coal because it produces greenhouse gases.
- Coal burning also produces oxides of sulphur and nitrogen, which cause acid rain.
- Cheaper coal can be imported from eastern Europe, the USA and Australia.

Questions

Economic decline

1 Refer to your own notes for an example of the decline of employment in a small area. This could be caused by something like the closure of a factory or a pit. The closure could have been due to a fall in demand for the product, exhaustion of a resource, lack of investment, etc.

2 Has the closure caused a downward spiral in other aspects of the area's geography?

3 Has anything been done to try to halt the downward spiral?

Economic development

> **Key idea 2**
> Some countries are emerging from a 'less economically developed' status.
> They can be classed as 'newly industrializing countries' (NICs). Economic
> development is linked to international interdependence.
>
> **Scale**
> *Regional*
> *International*
> *Global*
>
> **Expanded key idea**
> Most countries that have tried to develop their economies have felt that they need capital
> (money) to invest and markets to which they can export their products. Often the capital for
> investment has come from large transnational corporations. Trade can only increase if more
> wealthy countries agree to buy goods from the developing countries. Trade has sometimes
> been made easier for LEDCs by a series of international agreements and economic alliances.

Investment and development

Some people think that economies go through a series of stages as they
are developing. In order to move from one stage to another money must
be invested not only in plant and machinery, but also in **infrastructure**.
This means transport networks, development of power supplies, and so
on. Investment in the workforce, through education and training, is also
vital.

Stages of development: how investment is needed for economic growth

5 High mass consumption A wealthy
population can afford the many products
and services that the economy can produce.

4 Drive to maturity A large variety of
industries develop. The 'multiplier effect'
spreads growth to all regions of the country.

3 Take-off Profits produced by industry and
trade are invested in rapid growth of key
industries, like iron and steel. Growth is
concentrated in a few favoured regions.

2 Money comes from savings or from
outside the country to start investment in
infrastructure and development of simple
industry. This provides the **preconditions for
development.**

1 Traditional society The economy is based
on subsistence agriculture.

Hints and Tips!
You do not need
to learn this
diagram exactly
for use in the
exam. It has been
used here to help
you to understand
a difficult topic.

Where to find investment money

The model on the previous page is useful. The problem comes in seeing where a country can get the money it needs to invest, so that it can move through the stages. The model was based on countries in western Europe. They developed in the nineteenth century, using profits they had made from their colonies in Asia, Africa and South America. This trade had also provided capital for the USA to develop.

In the twentieth century the less economically developed countries (LEDCs) cannot use the wealth of other, weaker countries to provide their capital. They have to find money for investment from another source. Some hoped that they could get aid from the more economically developed countries (MEDCs), but this was never enough to allow them to reach the 'take-off' stage.

Many countries have had to rely on investment by large transnational companies (TNCs) to provide the money for their development. Brazil is one example where this has worked, to some extent. However, it has also caused some problems.

Case study

Brazil's path to development

By 1950 the South East region of Brazil had reached Stage 2 of the development model. The growth and export of coffee had led to the development of a good rail network around São Paulo and Rio de Janeiro. Banks and other financial services had developed, and there were a reasonable number of trained, educated people. The area also had valuable resources of iron ore, and a small steel industry had started.

However, population was growing quickly, and this meant that people could not save money to invest in 'take-off'. Money had to come in from outside. The government took a decision to try and attract investment by giving very favourable tax concessions to foreign firms. They thought that the motor industry would be particularly good for stimulating development.

Early investors included Ford and General Motors (USA), Fiat (Italy) and VW (Germany). The industry rapidly produced a multiplier effect, and stimulated growth in many parts of the economy of South East Brazil. Now the country ranks very highly in the world for its output:

Industry in Brazil	Cars	Steel	Aircraft	Ships
World ranking	9th	7th	6th	11th

◆ 1.3 billion people (23 per cent of the world's population) have less than $1 a day (66p) to live on. How can they hope to find money to invest in developing infrastructure?

◆ In the 1960s the United Nations agreed that all the MEDCs should aim to give 0.7 per cent of their GNP as aid to LEDCs. Most countries never achieved this aim. At present the UK gives about 0.2 per cent of GNP, but much of this is to buy goods from British firms.

ocus Point 1

In 1950 the São Paulo region had several advantages for development. List four of them.

ocus Point 2

Suggest how the growth of a skilled labour force in the motor industry helped the aircraft industry.

Suggest how the growth of the other industries created a market for shipbuilding.

Development of Brazil's car industry

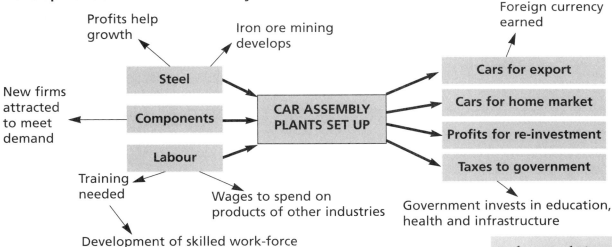

Key   ⟶ Inputs and outputs of car assembly plant
          ⟶ Multiplier effects on the rest of the economy

Other industries in Brazil

It also has important petrochemical, office machinery, computer and precision instrument industries. At first its industry relied on imported fossil fuels for power, but now it has many large HEP plants, and is developing nuclear and solar power. In order to reduce oil imports Brazil has developed cars that run on alcohol produced from sugar cane.

Many indicators show that Brazil is at least part way to becoming a mature industrial economy (Stage 4 on the model, page 105). GNP is $2680/person, the death rate is falling, and life expectancy has increased to 66 years. However, many problems remain.

Problems of Brazil's development

Brazil's 'economic miracle' of the 1960s and 1970s saw the economy grow by 10 per cent per year, but at a price:

- The country has huge foreign debts, which it may never be able to pay back.

- Inflation is very high – over 400 per cent per year in 1991.

- Growth has not been evenly spread. Industrialization is concentrated in the South East. This has led to massive migration (see page 92).

- Migration and urbanization have caused big social problems – housing shortages, underemployment, abandoned children, etc.

- To pay foreign debts, and to provide resources for the industry, large areas of rainforest have been cleared. Iron ore and other minerals are being developed for export. (See page 38.)

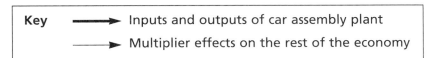

Hints and Tips!

You: 'I can't possibly learn all that. It's far too complicated.'

Author: 'Right. So break it down into easy stages. First learn the main inputs and outputs, which are boxed and printed in **bold**. Then use your common sense and your geographical understanding to work out the rest. The other labels show how each input stimulated other industries. Simple, really!'

To help you learn this list, divide it into three sections:

- economic problems
- social problems
- environmental problems.

- To provide power, several river basins have been flooded, again causing environmental problems.

In future Brazil must concentrate on spreading development to other regions, away from the South East. However, this development should be *sustainable* and not just exploit the environment; and it should be *for the benefit of all the people*, not just the very rich and powerful.

Remember the two phrases in *italics*. They may be useful to help you plan and structure an answer in your exam.

Free trade and protectionism

International trade should mean that each country benefits from the exchange. Each country specializes in producing and selling what it can do best. Then it sells what it can produce well and buys what it cannot produce well. Trade works best when both sides profit from the deal.

Free trade allows countries to export and import goods without interference from governments. People who believe in free trade think that it allows everyone to specialize in what they do best. Allowing competition makes sure that everyone benefits from efficient production.

Sometimes, though, countries set up barriers to free trade. For instance, in the 1960s British cotton producers could not make cloth as cheaply as Indians could. Imports from India threatened to put the British firms out of business. The UK government tried to protect the British firms. They put **tariffs** (taxes) on imported cotton, so that its price was the same as cotton produced in this country. They also set **quotas** on imports. These meant that only a certain amount of cloth was allowed into the country. This type of government action is called **protectionism**.

Unfortunately these tariffs and quotas had several damaging effects. They kept prices high for British consumers. They also stopped British firms trying to compete by becoming more efficient and cutting costs. Finally, they damaged the new industries in LEDCs because they stopped them from exporting.

International trade agreements

In order to encourage trade between countries, several international organizations and agreements have been set up. Some try to encourage all countries to trade freely. Others make special agreements between groups of countries.

GATT
The General Agreement on Tariffs and Trade is a world-wide agreement that tries to reduce protectionism and encourage free trade. A new agreement was signed in 1993. The USA was keen that Japan and the EU should reduce their tariffs which tried to keep out manufactured goods from big US corporations.

Most countries signed the agreement because they thought it would reduce protectionism and increase world trade. It would reduce the risk of a recession in world trade, and a recession could cause job losses in many MEDCs and a reduction of demand for the products of LEDCs.

Hints and Tips!

The ideas in this part of the syllabus are difficult. Try to understand them, but do not panic if you cannot. Questions on this section will never form more than a tiny part of the exam.

GATT also allows the NICs to develop, because it means they can sell the goods that they have been able to produce cheaply because of their lower labour costs. GATT does allow LEDCs to have tariffs for a few years, so that new industries can start up without being swamped by products from countries where industry is well established.

The EU

The European Union was set up after the Second World War to encourage trade between the former enemies in Europe. It was hoped that greater interdependence would lead to peace and stability in the future.

At first there were six member states, but by 1997 it had fifteen members, and it is planned to enlarge it further in the next few years. The organization has cut tariffs between member states and allows the free movement of goods, services and people. It has created a single market which is bigger than that of either the USA or Japan. By doing this it has increased trade, increased production and increased prosperity for most of its citizens.

The EU does have tariffs against imports from countries that are not in the EU. However, it has special trade agreements with some LEDCs. Most of these are former colonies of Britain, France and Belgium. They are allowed special deals when they export to the EU, especially for export of primary products. One example of these agreements is the import of bananas from former colonies such as Jamaica or Guadeloupe (see page 102). Unfortunately GATT has made this sort of deal illegal. It may not be possible to protect trade with small islands like this. Big US transnational corporations can produce bananas more cheaply, so small producers may be put out of business.

Other regional groups

The EU has been very successful. Other groups have been set up to try to encourage trade between member states (see map on next page), but none has gone so far as the EU yet. Many have cut some tariffs, but have not integrated their economies as EU countries have done.

OPEC

The Organization of Petroleum Exporting Countries represents the producers of the world's most important primary product. Many producers of raw materials feel that they get poor prices for their goods. OPEC is powerful enough to insist that importers pay a fair price for their raw materials. They are in this powerful position because:

- oil is vital to the economies of the MEDCs

- there are only limited supplies, so importers cannot look elsewhere for supplies.

Many other exporters of raw materials would like to set up organizations like OPEC, but usually their exports are not in such short supply, so they do not have the power to control prices.

Summary of main points about GATT:

- Encourages world trade.

- In theory everyone benefits because more trade means increased wealth.

- In fact some weaker, poor nations may lose out because big powerful countries and transnationals may dominate world trade even more than at present.

ocus Point 3

The EU has reduced tariffs to allow trade between certain countries. Which ones?

It has raised some tariffs to protect EU countries. From what?

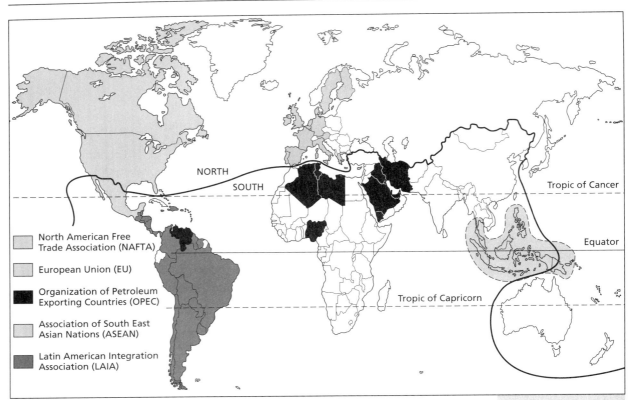

North American Free Trade Association (NAFTA)

European Union (EU)

Organization of Petroleum Exporting Countries (OPEC)

Association of South East Asian Nations (ASEAN)

Latin American Integration Association (LAIA)

NORTH
SOUTH

Tropic of Cancer

Equator

Tropic of Capricorn

▲ Groups of trading partners, and the 'north'/'south' divide

Exam practice

(a) Name one group of countries that has been set up to encourage trade between its members. (1 line 1 mark)

(b) Describe one of the policies of this group, and explain how it encourages trade. (5 lines 3 marks)

(c) To what extent have the policies of the group been successful? (5 lines 3 marks)

Trade and aid

> **Key idea 3**   **Scale**
> The gap between the wealthy 'north' and the poor 'south' is, in many cases,   *International*
> growing wider. Trade and aid are seen as agents of economic change.
>
> **Expanded key idea**
> Some less economically developed countries (LEDCs) have managed to develop their
> economies, either by exporting raw materials (OPEC countries like Saudi Arabia) or by
> developing industry (e.g. NICs like Taiwan and Brazil). However, many other LEDCs have
> achieved little, if any, development. In some the standard of living has fallen as population
> has increased faster than the economy. Trade and aid offer possible solutions to the
> increasing gap in wealth between the LEDCs and the MEDCs.

Measuring development

The figures in the graph below show the GNP per person for ten
countries. This means they show the average value of all the goods and
services produced by each person in the country.

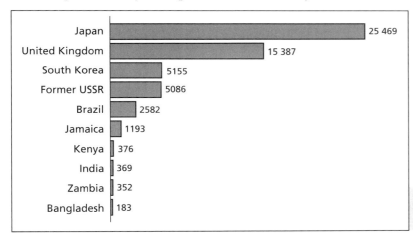

◀ *GNP (US$ per person) for
selected countries, 1993*

The top four on the graph are in the wealthy 'north', although there are
big differences between them. South Korea has only recently become a
more economically developed country and overtaken Russia.

The other six are in the poor 'south', although Brazil has started to
develop its industry, and to cross the 'income gap'. It is classified as a
newly industrializing country (NIC).

However, the graph only shows the GNP/person in one year. It should
be looked at together with the second graph on page 112 which shows
change in the GNP/person from 1990 to 1993.

The second graph shows:

- Japan and the UK had a high GNP and are continuing to grow.
- South Korea had quite a high GNP and is growing very fast.

Hints and Tips!

You do not need
to know the
precise GNPs of
the countries on
the graph, but it
may be useful to
know the names,
as examples of
economies that are
growing quickly,
growing slowly or
shrinking.

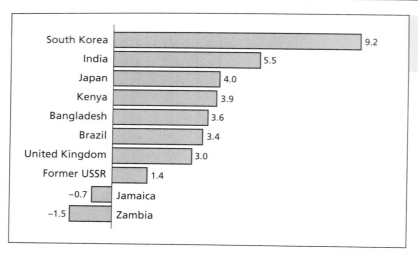

Percentage annual change in GNP (US$ per person) for selected countries, 1990–93

South Korea — 9.2
India — 5.5
Japan — 4.0
Kenya — 3.9
Bangladesh — 3.6
Brazil — 3.4
United Kingdom — 3.0
Former USSR — 1.4
Jamaica — −0.7
Zambia — −1.5

Hints and Tips!

Even if you do not learn what the graphs show, you may have to 'read' information from graphs like this in your exam.

- Russia had quite a high GNP but is only growing slowly.

- India, Kenya and Bangladesh had low GNPs and are growing quite fast, but they have a long way to go before they even reach Brazil's position.

- Jamaica and Zambia are poor, and becoming poorer over this period.

Some of the causes of these changes can be seen by looking at the cases of Kenya and Zambia, but first the fairness of trade should be examined.

Trade, change and development

When two people or two countries trade, both should benefit from the deal. This does not always happen, when one party in the deal is much weaker than the other. You may have seen fair and unfair trade at school.

International trade sometimes seems unfair too. Look at this example.

	LEDC	**MEDC**
Produces Needs	raw materials manufactured goods	manufactured goods raw materials

There seems to be a simple solution, so both countries get what they need:

But MEDCs have a lot of advantages in this trade:

- When raw materials are processed to make manufactured goods, the value increases. Manufactured goods are worth more than primary products.

- Many raw materials are produced by lots of different countries. The MEDCs can 'shop around' and try to get cheap prices.

- In many cases MEDCs can find substitutes if they cannot get primary products cheaply enough (for example sisal and pyrethrum in Kenya – see below).

- Many LEDCs are very dependent on exports of one single raw material. They have to take whatever price is offered, or they have no exports, so no income.

- Rich countries can afford to build up big stocks of raw materials, just in case any problems occur with the suppliers.

- LEDCs often depend on the MEDCs for the technology needed on their farms, plantations or mines.

So trade between the MEDCs and the LEDCs is not always very fair.

ocus Point 1

Cover the page, then list four advantages that MEDCs have, which make trade unfair.

Note You cannot do much about this 'unfair trade' – but some supermarkets are starting to stock some goods marked 'Fairtrade'. You can help poor people in poor countries by buying these goods.

Case study

Kenya's agriculture and European markets

There are three main farming systems in Kenya:

- pastoral subsistence farming in the dry north and east and in the Rift Valley, e.g. the Maasai

- arable subsistence farming in the wetter but remote west of Kenya, e.g. the Kikuyu

- commercial farming in the south, especially in the hill areas around Nairobi.

Subsistence farming
Attempts are being made to involve the subsistence farmers in the Kenyan economy. Small-scale aid projects encourage them to change

their farming practices in small ways so that they can produce a regular surplus for sale. Unfortunately this runs the risk of causing overfarming and soil erosion. Subsistence farmers may also become part of the modern economy by working in the tourist industry, as guides and rangers in the National Parks that are being set up in Kenya.

Commercial farming

The commercial farmers will make the biggest contribution to Kenya's trade in the foreseeable future. In the hills in the south of the country the climate is cooler and moister than in the rest of the country and soils are fairly fertile. These conditions attracted many European settlers when Kenya was a colony. They set up medium-sized plantations growing tea, coffee, sisal (which produces fibre for making rope) and pyrethrum (a flower that produces a natural insecticide).

The plantations used large numbers of Kenyan workers to produce crops, almost all for export. Britain was the main market, and provided most of the capital to set up the plantations and most of the managers to run them. Since Kenya became independent 35 years ago, native Kenyans have taken a bigger part in the running of the businesses, and this is likely to increase.

Unfortunately, the traditional products have fallen in value since Kenya became independent. There are many reasons, including:

- the demand for tea and coffee in MEDCs is not rising, but more countries are trying to produce them, so the price is falling
- machinery, fuel and fertilizer have to be imported, and the prices of these are going up
- the demand for sisal and pyrethrum is falling because synthetic chemicals can be used to make rope and pesticides.

Kenya has tried to maintain its profits from the plantations by:

- growing high-quality products to earn a better price
- trying to do more of the processing before the crop is exported, which also earns a better price
- emphasizing the 'natural' nature of its products, to appeal to the 'green' market
- improving conditions for plantation workers, to appeal to the 'fair trade' market.

Another way that Kenya has tried to increase the value of its agricultural exports is by moving into the expanding market for special vegetables. As consumers in MEDCs become more wealthy they are buying more 'exotic' vegetables. Things like mangetout peas, baby corn, okra, sweet potatoes and many more products are now found on many supermarket shelves in the UK. Many are grown in Kenya and then they are flown to Europe.

This new trade has brought revenue into Kenya but there are dangers:

Many gardeners now prefer to use natural insecticides, based on pyrethrum, rather than using chemical insecticides which can cause pollution.

ocus Point 2

Cover the page. List four problems that tropical plantations face in producing for international trade.

Give two ways that plantation owners try to overcome the problems.

- the crops have become fashionable – but they could fall out of fashion, so Kenya must not rely on them too much

- new crops are sometimes grown on land that was previously used for subsistence crops – so Kenya has increased its exports, but needs to import more food for its people.

Case study

Zambia's copper

Zambia is a land-locked country in southern Africa. In the north of the country there are enormous supplies of copper and other ores which were developed by British firms when Zambia was a colony.

Now Zambia's exports and imports are, in order of value:

Exports	Imports
Copper	Machinery
Zinc	Vehicles
Cobalt	Chemicals
Lead	Foodstuffs
Tobacco	Fuels and lubricants

Zambia is caught in the trap of exporting low-value raw materials and importing high-value manufactured goods. It has to export the bulky copper ore by rail through neighbouring countries, adding to transport costs. In the past these neighbours have suffered wars or political instability. This has made the railways unreliable, and damaged Zambia's trade.

The graph on page 111 shows that Zambia is a poor country. Its reliance on exports of primary products means that it is getting poorer.

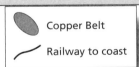
Copper Belt

Railway to coast

Focus Point 3

You could be asked to discuss whether it was right to grow exotic vegetables on land that was once used for growing subsistence crops.

Prepare the arguments for and against this.

Consider the views of various people and groups.

Questions

Aid

Refer to a case study of aid in an LEDC.

1 Who provides the money?

2 What new skills do the people learn?

3 Good aid projects build on the traditions of the area, rather than trying to change the whole way of life. Does your example fit this description?

Focus Point 4

Suggest why tobacco might not be a good crop to rely on in future.

Exam practice

(a) Describe an example of a successful aid project in an LEDC.
(8 lines 5 marks)

(b) Explain what made this aid project successful.   (8 lines 5 marks)

Tourism

> ### Key idea 4
>
> Tourism is seen as a way of creating economic growth, although it is difficult   **Scale**
> to ensure maximum benefit for local people.   *National*
> *International*
> *Global*
>
> ### Expanded key idea
>
> Tourism has been the world's fastest-growing industry during the last 30 years, and it will
> soon be the world's biggest source of employment. Much of the industry's recent growth has
> been in less economically developed countries (LEDCs), but the structure of the industry
> means that a large part of the money spent on holidays goes back to the more economically
> developed countries (MEDCs) and not to the people of the LEDC.

Tourism and development

The tourist industry has grown rapidly since the development of
aeroplanes which allow cheap, international transport. It has become
fashionable for tourists to travel to more distant parts of the world.
Some LEDCs have become popular destinations because of their
climate, scenery, exotic culture and low prices.

The governments of the LEDCs have often encouraged the
development of resorts in their countries. They see it as a way of
bringing money into the country. This will help to modernize the
country's infrastructure and bring jobs and foreign currency. It will also
help to produce a modern work-force, and encourage training and
education. It is hoped that new skills that are developed will be
transferable to other industries.

Quite clearly the tourist industry has brought benefits to many LEDCs,
but it has also had costs. To understand why the benefits have often
been less than was hoped it is important to understand the structure of
the tourist industry.

ocus Point 1

Cover the page. List
four benefits that
tourism might bring
to the economy of
an LEDC.

The cost structure of the tourist industry

Imagine that a family spent £1000 on a holiday in an LEDC like Tunisia.
The table opposite shows where the money might go.

Once the family arrive in Tunisia they will spend money on trips,
souvenirs, drinks in cafés, and so on. Some of this money will also go
into the local economy, but some will go as profits to transnational
firms that have invested in the LEDC. So the tourist industry does not
bring great benefits to the poor in the country that is visited. In fact,
most of the money and profits go to MEDCs.

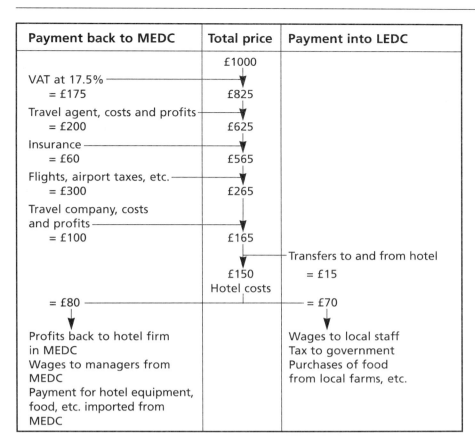

Payment back to MEDC	Total price	Payment into LEDC
	£1000	
VAT at 17.5% = £175	↓ £825	
Travel agent, costs and profits = £200	↓ £625	
Insurance = £60	↓ £565	
Flights, airport taxes, etc. = £300	↓ £265	
Travel company, costs and profits = £100	↓ £165	
	↓ £150 Hotel costs	Transfers to and from hotel = £15
= £80 ↓		= £70 ↓
Profits back to hotel firm in MEDC Wages to managers from MEDC Payment for hotel equipment, food, etc. imported from MEDC		Wages to local staff Tax to government Purchases of food from local farms, etc.

Other costs and benefits of the tourist industry

Apart from the financial benefits, shown above, the tourist industry can have other effects on the life of a country.

Costs	Benefits
The construction of hotels, roads, airports, etc. can damage the local environment.	Infrastructure, such as roads, can also be used by people.
Tourists sometimes do not respect local culture and traditions, e.g. Muslim codes of dress.	Local culture and traditions can be supported by tourism, e.g. dancing for tourists.
Beaches can be closed to local people because tourists want exclusive use.	People who work in the tourist industry receive education and training.
Tourists demand comforts which can overuse local resources, such as water supplies.	Development of water resources and sanitation for tourists may also benefit local people.
Local people may lose confidence when they see so many tourists who are all so much richer than they are.	Presence of outsiders in the country may encourage respect for civil rights and equal opportunities.

Hints and Tips!

This table illustrates an important idea, but it is not necessary to learn the figures in detail.

When LEDCs set up tourist industries they all want to encourage wealthy holiday-makers. Hundreds of student backpackers used to visit Nepal, but they took very little money with them. The country was keen to encourage organized groups, who wanted better conditions, but who would pay well for them.

Focus Point 2

Cover the page. List five items of tourist expenditure that stay in the LEDC.

List five ways that money 'leaks' back to MEDCs.

The tourist industry depends on fashion. At the moment a new resort may be fashionable, but it might easily lose favour. For instance, political problems (as in Egypt) or natural disasters (hurricanes in the Caribbean) can ruin a country's tourism. So can economic problems in MEDCs. If there is a slump in the European economy, the first thing that people give up is their exotic, long-distance holiday. The LEDCs can do little to control this.

Finally, the growth of tourism can destroy the environment that made the country attractive in the first place. Sometimes the profits from tourism can be used for environmental conservation (for example Kenya's National Parks). Unfortunately the tourist industry grows too big too quickly in some places. Then the massive developments can cause pollution of air, sea and the visual environment. Once this happens the industry moves on to another place, leaving the LEDC damaged but not developed.

Questions

Tourism

1 Name an example of an LEDC that has tried to develop its tourist industry.

2 Describe its location and attractions.

3 What infrastructure developments have taken place?

4 Describe some of the benefits and problems brought by tourism.

◆ Many people in Egypt welcome tourists, but some fundamentalists want to stop foreign tourism. In 1997 there were a number of massacres of tourists. Obviously this frightened many people and had a disastrous effect on the tourist industry.

◆ Natural disasters do not always destroy tourism. The eruption of the Mount St Helens volcano in the USA brought a big growth in tourism. The eruption gave a lot of free publicity to the area's spectacular scenery.

◆ Bermuda is trying to develop a tourist industry, attracting cruise liners from the USA. Unfortunately this small island has only a very limited water supply. The cruise liners now have to bring their own supply of water for the tourists.

Exam questions

Advice on answering multiple choice questions

• You can work out the answer by guessing.	• Pure guessers will only be right once every five guesses. Good geographers will do far better than this.
• There is sometimes more than one right answer.	• No there isn't. Some answers may be nearly right, but they are not the best answers. These 'nearly right' answers are called 'distracters'. Be careful you do not get distracted and pick the wrong answer. The difference between the right answer and a distracter is very subtle – maybe just one word.
• You cannot prepare for this sort of question.	• Yes you can. Some questions test facts that can be learned. Some test ideas that you should know. Others test skills that you can practise.
• Some people have a knack for doing these. Others just don't and will never be able to learn.	• You could say there is a knack in all kinds of exam question. This paper rewards people who are good at clear, precise analysis, but it does not test the ability to write well. Both types of skill are important, and writing is tested on Paper 2. People often improve their skill on this paper, with practice. Below are some tips for improvement.

Multiple choice questions arouse strong feelings in some teachers and students. Some people love them and others hate them.

Advantages
There are several advantages of these types of question:

- The questions are short and quick. This means that it is possible to cover all the key ideas in the syllabus.

- Questions can be carefully pre-tested and standardized. This means that the level of difficulty of each question can be tested in advance. Only questions that are moderate and quite easy will go on the Foundation paper. Only moderate and difficult ones will go on the Higher paper. (There will be some overlap to allow comparison.)

- Using standardized questions makes it easier to check on grade standards from one year to the next.

Tips
Here are some tips to help you get the most marks you possibly can.

- Practise by using as many past papers as possible. Certain styles of question come up on many papers. Try to get used to them.

- You must follow the instructions on the paper very carefully. They are marked by computer, which only gives you the mark if you have done exactly what you are told to do.

- Always read the question very, very carefully. One word can make the difference between the right answer and a distracter.

- Do not panic. People rarely run out of time on this paper. If, at first, you cannot do a question, stop; think; re-read it. Work out *exactly* which part of the syllabus is being tested. Work out *exactly* what the key words mean. As you consider this carefully, things may suddenly fall into place. Do not, though, spend too long on any one question. If you are stuck with a question, leave it and come back to it later.

- There are two ways of working out the right answer. Either pick the one you think is correct, or rule out all the ones you think are wrong. The clever student does it both ways – pick what you think is right, then check that all the others are wrong.

- Write on the question paper if you need to. <u>Underline</u> key words and phrases in the **instructions**. Mark the 5 choices of answer: '✗' = wrong answer, '✓' = right answer, '?' = not sure, come back to this. (Your teacher might object to this, because the paper may be needed for next year's mocks – but your real exam is more important just now!)

- If you have tried everything else, and you are still not sure of the correct answer, you must guess. You will not lose marks if you are wrong, and you have a chance if you put something down.

- Be clever about your guessing, though. Narrow the odds. A pure guess has one chance in five, which is not a good bet, so try to rule out some of the possible answers. If you know that two of them are wrong you are picking one from three. That gives you a lot more chance of a correct answer than one from five.

- Never, *never*, NEVER underline more than one answer to a question. There is only one right answer, and you will automatically be marked wrong if you underline two – even if one of them was correct.

- As you go through the paper, keep checking the question numbers and the answer numbers. It is quite easy to slip onto the wrong line on the answer sheet, and then get all your answers muddled up.

- Throughout the paper stay calm and logical. The multiple completion questions at the end look complicated, but the geography they test is no more difficult than in the earlier questions.

Questions

Multiple choice questions

Each of the questions **1** to **9** is followed by five responses A, B, C, D and E. For each question select the best response and mark its letter on the answer sheet.

1 'This used to be a really friendly working-class area. We had all grown up together, and we helped each other out when times got hard. Then all these young businessmen moved in, and businesswomen. The skips arrived, they stripped the old furniture and decorations and tarted them up with their extensions and pot plants. When they turned the local pub into a wine bar we knew it was time for us to move out. It wasn't our area any more.'
   What name is given to the process described above?
   A slum clearance
   B inner city redevelopment
   C gentrification
   D suburbanization
   E counterurbanization   (Page 21)

2 Which letter, A–E, has two statements that are **both** true?
   A Japan is on a constructive margin   California is on a destructive margin
   B Japan is on a slip margin   California is on a destructive margin
   C Japan is on a destructive margin   California is on a constructive margin
   D Japan is on a destructive margin   California is on a slip margin
   E Japan is on a constructive margin   California is on a slip margin   (Pages 64–68)

3 What name is given to the area of calm at the centre of a storm?
   A the vortex
   B the eye
   C the cumulus
   D the willy-willy
   E each one has a different name, all in alphabetical order   (Pages 69–71)

4 'The present inhabitants of the Earth should do their best to look after the planet's resources and leave the Earth in a good condition for future generations.'
   Which word, A–E, best describes the idea in the quotation above?
   A development
   B exploitation
   C redevelopment
   D attitude
   E stewardship   (Page 84)

5 Which of these is a true statement about the present steel industry in the EU?
   A There are no steelworks left in Germany.
   B All the integrated steelworks are by deepwater ports.
   C The steel industry has spread as the EU has expanded.
   D Most large EU steelworks are located near to iron ore deposits.
   E There are fewer steelworks now than there were in 1960.   (Pages 94–97)

6 Which of these shops would you be most likely to find in a small group of shops on a suburban housing estate?
   A Men's fashions
   B Newsagent and sweet shop
   C Department store
   D Electrical goods
   E Furniture showroom   (Pages 100–101)

7

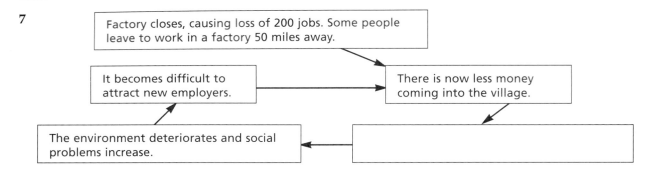

| Factory closes, causing loss of 200 jobs. Some people leave to work in a factory 50 miles away. |
| It becomes difficult to attract new employers. |
| There is now less money coming into the village. |
| The environment deteriorates and social problems increase. |

Which sentence best fits in the empty box in the spiral of decline shown above?
A Many employers are attracted by the skilled work-force.
B The area gets grants from the EU to improve the environment.
C Local shops and services close down.
D New shops are opened to try and boost the economy.
E The area becomes an 'industrial heritage park'.   *(Page 104)*

8 Which of the following phrases best explains why it is difficult to start industrialization in LEDCs?
A Transnationals want to invest in LEDCs and take all the profits.
B LEDCs are short of the necessary raw materials.
C In most LEDCs it is difficult to provide/find capital to start industry.
D Wage rates are too high in LEDCs.
E LEDCs suffer severe shortages of labour because most people work on farms.
                                              (Pages 105–108)

9 Which of these sentences describes a problem that is often found in LEDCs when the tourist industry is developed there?
A As the industry grows it damages the unspoilt environment that first attracted the tourists.
B The standard of living falls for all the local people.
C Airports in MEDCs charge high prices in their souvenir shops.
D Terrorists often attack tourists, which gives LEDCs a bad reputation.
E The standard of living improves for some of the people.   *(Pages 116–118)*

Matching pairs questions

In questions **10–24**, each group of questions has a set of responses A, B, C, D and E. In each group each letter may be used once, more than once, or not at all. For each question select the best response and mark its letter on the answer sheet.

Questions 10–14
Five features are marked A–E on this diagram of limestone scenery. Which letter shows:

10 a swallow hole
11 a spring or resurgence
12 a limestone pavement
13 a stalagmite
14 a bedding plane?

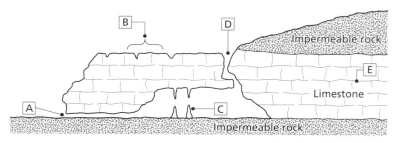

                                                              (Page 43)

Questions 15–19

These are definitions of features or processes of a river basin:

A   a small river that joins a larger river
B   the place where a river joins the sea
C   the line that marks the edge of a river basin
D   the place where a river starts
E   a place where two rivers join.

Which description, A–E, defines:

15   a river's source
16   a watershed
17   a tributary
18   a confluence
19   a river mouth.   (*Page 47*)

Questions 20–24

This diagram shows inputs and outputs of a market garden in the Netherlands.

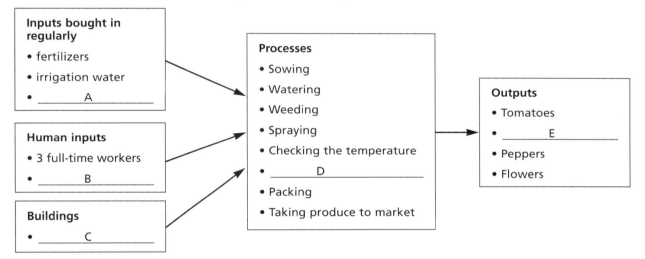

Which letter should each of these words or phrases be matched with?

20   Cucumbers
21   Greenhouses
22   Harvesting
23   Part-time workers
24   Seeds   (*Pages 61–62*)

Multiple completion questions

In each of the questions **25–31**, one or more of the responses is/are correct. Decide which of the responses is/are correct and mark A, B, C, D or E on the answer sheet as follows.
A if (1) alone is correct.
B if (1) and (2) are correct.
C if (1), (2) and (3) are all correct.
D if (2) and (3) are correct.
E if (3) alone is correct.

Summarized directions				
A	**B**	**C**	**D**	**E**
(1) only	(1) and (2)	(1) (2) and (3)	(2) and (3)	(3) only

25 Which of the following is/are true?
(1) There is a shortage of labour in many cities in LEDCs, which means poor people migrate there to fill vacant jobs.
(2) Most of the world's fastest-growing cities are in MEDCs.
(3) Rapid urbanization is happening in many parts of South America and Africa.   (*Pages 7–9*)

26 Immigrants who move into cities in the UK and other MEDCs often live in the inner city, close to other people from the same ethnic group. Why?
(1) Old inner city housing is fairly cheap, so new migrants can afford a place to live.
(2) Other people from the same ethnic group live here and can provide support and help new migrants settle in the country.
(3) Many new migrants get jobs in old industries in the inner city, or in public transport which has depots in the inner city.   (*Pages 23–25*)

27 Which of these are essential parts of a soil that is good for farming?
(1) air and water
(2) minerals and humus
(3) organisms, like bacteria and worms   (*Page 56*)

28 Which of the following statements about tropical storms is/are true?
(1) Tropical storms start over the sea.
(2) Most tropical storms start in late summer or early autumn.
(3) Tropical storms gain force when they reach the land.   (*Page 69*)

29 Which of these UK steelworks is/are situated on the coast?
(1) Port Talbot
(2) Redcar, Teesside
(3) Scunthorpe   (*Pages 95–96*)

30 Which of the statements below help(s) to explain why the M4 Corridor has become an important area for high-tech industry?
(1) There is a large supply of cheap labour in the East End of London.
(2) There is easy access to Heathrow and Gatwick airports so the M4 Corridor is accessible to contacts from all round the world.
(3) There are many universities and research centres nearby.   (*Pages 97–99*)

31 Three shops each have a threshold population population of 10 000 people.
(1) 11 000 people live within range.
(2) 10 000 people live within range.
(3) 9000 people live within range.
Which shop, or shops, will make a profit and survive?   (*Pages 100–101*)

Exam practice answers

Page 15

(a) There are 4 marks available and you have to write about push factors and pull factors. This probably means 2 marks for pushes and 2 marks for pulls. You will only get the second mark for each if you elaborate and develop an idea in detail. For example:

'People are pushed from the countryside by a shortage of jobs.' = 1 mark.

'People are pushed from the countryside because mechanization has cut the number of workers needed on the land.' = 2 marks

(b) This question is about building spontaneous settlements. Describe your case study in detail. Write about real places that you have studied. Try not to write in very general terms that could refer to *any* settlement in *any* LEDC in the world.

(c) Write a clear definition and then provide some examples:

'The informal sector is work that is done by individuals or small groups who do not work for a large firm. Hours are often irregular. The businesses do not have much equipment, and people often work from home. Recycling waste, making things to sell on the street, or doing odd building jobs for neighbours are all examples.'

Page 19

The Burgess model showed that housing did get better as one moved out from the city centre – but the model was a big simplification. In many towns and cities it would be true to say:

'On average, housing quality improves with distance from the centre, but some areas do not fit the pattern.'

There are two key points to writing a good answer to this question.

1 You need precise knowledge about different areas of your named town or city. Most people will write about the area they live in, or one they visit regularly.

2 The answer must be carefully planned. Mention old inner city housing and newer, modern suburban development which probably fit the pattern. Then mention areas of inner city regeneration, or poor housing on the edge of town, which probably do not fit the pattern.

Page 34

For each of your chosen topics you should:

(i)   State clearly where you are writing about.

(ii) Describe how the area has changed. (You may well divide this section into benefits and problems – good changes and bad ones.)

(iii) Explain how this change can be linked to changes in transport.

(iv) You might give a brief summary saying whether *you* think the changes have benefited the area.

Page 38

There are three topics to write about, and each one could refer to both people and environment. Therefore you must plan your answer very carefully. It is probably easiest to stick to the order of topics in the question. You will only get high-level marks if you have links and elaborations in your answer. For instance, here are two extracts showing student answers to the first part of this question:

Student answer	Examiner's comment
'Exposed soil has no vegetation cover.✓ There are no roots growing in the soil.✓ This can lead to soil erosion.✓ It ruins the environment✓ and farmers cannot grow crops without soil.'✓	I can see 5 correct points, which I have ticked, but they are very simple ideas. They are not linked or elaborated.
'If vegetation is removed there are no roots to hold the soil together and no leaves to protect it from raindrop impact. Soil can be eroded, leaving the farmland without any nutrients for crop growth. It leaves the environment looking bare and unattractive.	This answer explains why loss of roots and leaves lets rain erode the soil. Then it explains, briefly but correctly, how this damages people and the environment. It is part of a high-level answer – much better than the first example.

Page 52

(a) (i)   arable, capital intensive, commercial
    (ii)   arable, labour intensive, near subsistence
    (iii) market gardening, capital and labour intensive, commercial.

(b) (i)   pastoral, extensive, near subsistence
    (ii)   pastoral/mixed, capital intensive, commercial
    (iii) market gardening, capital intensive, commercial.

Page 78

Whenever you have to 'Choose . . . ', read the whole question before you choose. This is important because you must pick an example that allows you to write good answers to all parts of the question.

(a) *Low-level* answers will include things like *'the climate is hot and dry'.*
Middle-level answers will be more precise, e.g. *'The summers are hotter than in England, and are almost guaranteed free from rain in August.'*
High-level answers use statistics: *'Average July temperatures are 21°C and average July rainfall is less than 20mm, compared with about 16°C and 40mm in Cornwall.'*

(b) The question asks for a list and only allows three lines. So stick to a list of three named buildings or facilities. Do not waste time elaborating your answer.

(c) This question asks you to *explain*. You must give facts, and then elaborate them. In your answer you should have phrases like:

'... this happens *because* ...' '... this is a *result of* ...' '... this *leads to* ...', and so on.

Page 83

The key to a good answer to this question is to link *knowledge* with an *appreciation of people's values*. For instance:

- The car salesman obviously needs oil to be supplied, or he could not make a living – so link that to the fact that the USA is the world's biggest consumer of oil.

- The fisherman needs unpolluted fishing grounds, so link that with specific details about the *Exxon Valdez* disaster.

- The tribe might worry about the pipeline affecting traditional hunting grounds, but they would also benefit from jobs – but then how long would these jobs last? Keep thinking things through and debating different points.

Page 91

(a)

Stage	1	2	3	4
Death rate	high	starts to fall	still falling	low
Birth rate	high	high	starts to fall	low
Total population	low	rising at an increasing rate	still rising, but at a slower rate	high, but now stable

Award 1 mark each time birth rate and death rate are both correct in a stage. 4×1

Award 1 mark for each correct population total. 4×1

(b) Death rate starts to fall/because of new medical discoveries. 2×1

(c) Birth rate starts to fall/because couples see benefits in limiting family size. 2×1

In (b) and (c) the first mark is for a simple correct statement. The second mark is for elaboration or explanation.

Page 110

(a) Give a mark for any of the groups mentioned in the chapter, except OPEC.

(b) & (c)   Both parts need brief answers.
1 mark given for any point that is relevant and correct.
2 marks for some elaboration or explanation.
3 marks for a clear or detailed elaboration, or for a good example of how the organization works. For example, in (b):

'GATT has been a success for the MEDCs. It has encouraged increased trade, and all the economies of Europe and North America have expanded. It has been less successful at helping poor countries industrialize, because they cannot protect new industries by putting up tariffs against imports.'

Page 115

(a) You must try to be specific and write in detail about a real place.
1–2 marks Some details are given, but the answer lacks precision. There may be no place or country named.
3–4 marks The answer is reasonably precise. Several simple points are made, or at least one point is developed and elaborated.
5 marks There is a clear sense of place in the answer. Several detailed points are made and linked together.

(b) You are asked to 'explain' here. Give reasons for what you write. For example:

'Water harvesting in Mali did not try to totally change the way of life of local people – it just tried to improve water supply to the subsistence crops. The only materials used, stones, could be found locally, and the project made use of local labour, so people felt that it was their "own" project.'

Answers

Answers to multiple choice questions, matching pairs and multiple completion questions

1 = C	8 = C	14 = E	20 = E	26 = C
2 = D	9 = A	15 = D	21 = C	27 = C
3 = B	10 = D	16 = C	22 = D	28 = B
4 = E	11 = A	17 = A	23 = B	29 = B
5 = E	12 = B	18 = E	24 = A	30 = D
6 = B	13 = C	19 = B	25 = E	31 = B
7 = C				

Index